THE BASICS OF
STOCKS

Gerald Krefetz

Dearborn
Financial Publishing, Inc.

Publisher: Kathleen A. Welton
Associate Editor: Karen A. Christensen
Senior Project Editor: Jack L. Kiburz
Interior Design: Lucy Jenkins
Cover Design: Sam Concialdi

Published by Dearborn Financial Publishing, Inc.

Printed in the United States of America

94 10 9 8 7 6 5 4 3

Library of Congress Cataloging-in-Publication Data

Krefetz, Gerald.
    The basics of stocks / Gerald Krefetz.
        p. cm. — (Making the most of your money series)
    Includes index.
    ISBN 0-79310-359-2 (paper)
    1. Stocks — United States. 2. Investments — United States.
  3. Stock-exchange — United States. I. Title. II. Series: Krefetz,
  Gerald. Making the most of your money series.
HG4921.K72 1992   91–42812
332.63'22—dc20   CIP

Dedication

To Dorothy, Nadine and Adriene

Contents

Introduction

Anyone considering investment in the stock market should be aware that it is subject to volatility. That, of course, has been the history of common stock since the first shares of the East India Company and the Hudson Bay Company were traded in 17th-century England and *publick stock* (government bonds) was exchanged after the American Revolution.

Indeed, market fluctuations are as old as history, whether the items are shares, bonds or commodities. Of late, volatility has increased. In the years following the October 1987 crash, when the Dow Jones Industrial Average (DJIA) lost 508 points and the Standard & Poor's 500 (S&P 500) lost 16.22 in one day, there were a half-dozen occasions when the stock market swung back and forth 100 points on the DJIA and 6 on the S&P 500. But periods of volatility were followed by periods of quietude, just as night follows day.

Savers and investors must consider this a fact of financial life and not panic at scare headlines and alarmist broadcasts. No doubt easier said than done. The old saw "If all about you are losing their heads, and you aren't, you may not understand the situation" perhaps has some truth to it. By and large, actions conditioned by panic are seldom successful. For example, investors who panicked and dumped their securities on "meltdown" Monday, or shortly thereafter, in retrospect suffered considerably. Six months later, the broad market averages had recovered substantially—somewhere between 15 and 40 percent, depending on which average is used as a baseline.

Unhappily, many individuals sustained major damage to their nest eggs. Some were in highly leveraged positions and faced margin calls (in other words, they had to deposit funds or securities to maintain the minimum ratio of debt to equity). Others were on the wrong side of derivative instruments (for example, options and futures) that either expired worthless or created enormous exposures that eventually had to be covered at great cost. Perhaps the chief reason for tragic losses—losses of funds accumulated over a lifetime—was the lack of balance and diversification. Too many investors did not take the trouble to establish safe and secure savings programs before starting an investment program. Had they done so, even a poorly planned and disastrously executed investment program would not have left them bereft of their life savings.

Will investors ever recover their nerve after Black Monday and this wild wave of volatility? Is it still possible to make money in the face of a new tax code and inflationary forces? Can individual investors with modest funds compete with institutional megabuck investors in an era of programmed trading, where computers systematically trade baskets of stocks?

The answers to these and related questions become apparent if we appraise what recently happened and put it in perspective. Since the October 19, 1987, crash has attained a historical importance similar to that of the October 1929 collapse, it is particularly important to view the 1987 market crash in a historical context.

Whether the 1987 crash ended the bull market is a matter of some dispute, but there is general agreement as to the beginning of the bull market. To prop up a tottering Mexican banking system in the summer of 1982, the Federal Reserve Board flooded the domestic and world economy with cash. In October, Paul Volcker, chairman of the Fed, announced that the Federal Reserve Board was indeed easing credit. This liquidity, directly and indirectly, made its way into the securities markets, joining the surplus cash previously made available for investment as a consequence of the 1981 tax cuts.

As the economy recovered from the 1982 recession, the stage was set for a long, prosperous and profitable economic recovery. From the summer of 1982 the stock market advanced as interest rates fell from the towering levels of the early Eighties. The bull market continued until the summer of 1987. Depending on which index you use, in the course of the five-year advance (1982 to 1987), the markets rose threefold without any real decline.

Perhaps it should have been no surprise that the market, eventually did what it always has done—it retreated after a long climb. Whether the country was about to enter a recession or the subsequent market decline would trigger a recession was debated long after the crash. But it was obvious that the business cycle, celebrating its fifth birthday that summer, was old by most standards (the average period of economic expansion in this century is 38 months).

When the crash came, the DJIA fell from its August high of 2,722 to 1,739 (with an intraday low of 1,615 on October 20), and the S&P 500, from 337 to 225. Whether you measure by the narrower gauge (DJIA) or the broader one (S&P 500), the market fell between 36 and 33 percent in a few weeks. Most analysts suggest that a fall of more than 20 percent constitutes a bear market. Whatever the name, the drop was certainly a "cold shower," not only riveting attention to the markets, the financial mechanisms and the new trading techniques that had sprung up during the course of the bull market, but also reiterating the fact that markets are two-way streets. When they become over-valued, they invariably sell off.

Moreover, the crash destroyed the complacency that long bull markets breed. One could no longer make money by buying virtually anything. Reality brought with it a discriminating, back-to-basics sense, whether of the fundamental or technical persuasion. There were other consequences as well, which shall be examined later. But the question of how the crash immediately affected the market in terms of short-term and long-term performance is on the whole optimistic. Economists, financial observers and the media, however, like to harp on the idea that $500 billion to $1 trillion were lost in the Crash of 1987.

These are highly misleading figures, because measurements are based on losses suffered from market tops. Put it another way, calculating losses from the top down assumes that peak prices are average or sustainable values. If markets are to be measured by the most marginal buyer or seller—the most emotional, whether driven by greed or fear—then evaluations are likely to be extreme, if not bizarre. Much money was lost on Black Monday, but it serves no purpose to exaggerate those claims.

In fact, the S&P 500 industrials ended the year up by about 4 percent. On average, it appears that most investors lost most of their return for the year. No doubt some lost more, and a few lost their entire bankroll. But most investors, especially the long-term ones, fared well enough. Had they started an investment program on the first day of 1980, an unmanaged portfolio of securities as measured by the S&P 500 would have risen by 130 percent (plus dividends) by January 1, 1988. Not too shabby!

Meltdown Monday offers a number of lessons that anyone interested in the health of his or her wealth should seriously consider. Among these, one lesson seems abundantly clear: Long-term investors with balanced, diversified portfolios of stocks, bonds and savings survived.

Indeed, they not only survived but also continued to earn interest on fixed-income accounts and regained much of their losses. At the same time, they emerged with sounder portfolios. Passing the scene of a car crash doesn't necessarily make you a safer driver, but it certainly will make you reflect a while on the consequences of not driving safely.

• 1 •

How To Get Started

WHAT KIND OF INVESTOR ARE YOU?

Before investing your first dollar, it helps to understand what kind of investor you are. Understanding your objectives and your own nature is a large part of successful investing. You can define these by determining your time frame and what sort of yield you are seeking within that period.

Time Frame

Are you investing for short-term, medium-term or long-term objectives? If you have indeed previously invested, a glance at your transactions will reveal your tactics, though perhaps not your intentions. Short-term speculations have a way of becoming long-term investments when the market moves the wrong way.

By definition, successful investing is a long-range endeavor. If you are the kind of person who expects immediate results and instant gratification, you are by temperament unsuited to long-term investment. The financial markets are basically a reflection of the business world and its activities. Change in business conditions, product lines and profit margins can be slow. It takes time to turn around an ailing company or to enhance the prospects of a successful one. Therefore, investing is a waiting game, one in which success requires more patience than money.

Long-term investing can mean different things to different people, but in the financial world, long-term commitments are ones made for at least five years; middle-range investments are those between one and five years; and short-term commitments start tomorrow and last for a matter of months or a year or two.

Return on Investment

How long an investment is held is only one part of the equation. The more significant aspect is the percent of return on your money, or return on investment (ROI), which is fundamental to successful money management. Before considering how ROI applies to common stock, it is useful to look at some examples of *common* return on money. Though parameters are forever changing, it is possible to measure monetary yields.

The return on money—its yield—depends on two items: (1) the legislated rate, whether a floor or ceiling, and (2) the rate as determined by unregulated money markets. Since the deregulation of the financial world in the early 1980s, most legislated rates and restrictions have ended. In savings (demand) accounts, banks are no longer required to pay a set rate, though between 5.0 and 5.5 percent is now most common. (For a brief period in the mid-1980s, rates dipped below 5 percent at some banks.) Banks may—and many do—pay higher rates for money market accounts and time deposits such as certificates of deposit. Remember that in the 1970s money market accounts paid less interest than savings accounts.

In short, demand deposits, whether a savings account or a checking account that pays interest (a NOW account), usually provide a floor for interest rates with perfect safety, since these accounts in insured banks are guaranteed up to $100,000 by the FDIC. (Treasury bills, notes and bonds have virtually the same governmental guarantee, but the prices of these instruments vary and the promised principal may not be in-hand for many years, unless sold in the secondary market.)

If the yield on demand savings marks the low end of the yield spread, what determines the high end? The answer is that yield or return on money is directly proportionate to the amount of risk the owner of the funds is willing to accept—and the greater the risk, the greater the reward. A glance at money rates in the business section of the newspaper reveals that when the key money market rates are

Discount Rate	5 1/2
Prime Rate	8 1/2
Federal Funds	5 1/2
Treasury Bills (3 mos.)	5 1/2
Call Money	8

safe investments yield the following returns:

Certificate of Deposit (3 mos.)	5 3/8
Money Market Accounts	5
Money Market Mutual Funds	5 3/8
Super NOW Accounts	4 1/2
U.S. Savings Bonds	6 1/2

On the wilder shores, one might obtain the following:

Best-Grade Bonds	8 1/2
Intermediate-Grade Bonds	9
Junk Bonds	14+
Second Mortgages	15+

One can find companies whose common stock is momentarily paying dividends of 15 to 20 percent, but whose ability to continue paying at that rate (or any rate) ranges from problematic to highly doubtful. The higher the yield, the greater the danger that yield, principal, or both, are in jeopardy.

RETURN ON COMMON STOCK

The yield on fixed-income investments such as savings accounts, CDs, savings bonds and money market funds are rather straightforward, since the original principal is always returned, plus the accumulated interest. With bonds, the interest rate, or coupon rate, determines what the bond will yield. If bought at par value and redeemed at the same par value at maturity, the interest rate remains the same over the life of the bond. Should the bond be bought at a premium over or a discount under its face value, then the yield to maturity may be less or more than its coupon rate.

For common stock, the return on your capital must take into account not only the time over which the investment is held, but two other factors as well: the price at which it was acquired and the price at which it is subsequently sold (the profit), plus the dividend. This is called the holding period return (HPR) or holding period yield. The following simple formula can be applied either before a purchase (as a projection of return) or after the stock is sold to see precisely how well the investment performed. Thus:

$$HPR = \frac{\text{Dividend} + \text{Sold price} - \text{Buy price}}{\text{Buy price}}$$

$$HPR = \frac{D + P' - P}{P}$$

If the purchase price was $25 and you sold the shares for $30 one year later, and the dividend was $1, your holding period return would be 24 percent (minus commissions).

$$\frac{1 + 30 - 25}{25} = \frac{6}{25} = 24\%$$

The holding period return can easily be projected for fixed-income investments for which there is only one possible return of principal. For stock, the projection is obviously uncertain—indeed, there may even be a negative return should the share price go down. If you sell at a loss, the holding period return is a negative number. Even the dividend may be changed unexpectedly. The greater the uncertainty, the greater the risk attendant on the shares. The holding period return on utility and telephone company shares is far more predictable, hence less risky, than shares of initial public offerings—to cite two extremes.

It is important to understand the concept of HPR, or yield, since it allows you to quickly calculate comparisons between different companies' shares, as well as between stocks and other fixed-interest investments. (Bond yields are calculated somewhat differently from bank yields. This subject is discussed in another book in this series, *The Basics of Bonds*.) The holding period return quite simply shows you how much money, in percentage terms, your invested money is earning.

Two further considerations will be mentioned but not explored. Though there is no longer a difference between dividend income and capital gains income under the new tax code, there is still a considerable difference if the income is from a tax-free source (such as municipal bonds), or if the funds are invested in a tax-advantaged account (such as an IRA or other pension account). Furthermore, these yields are not adjusted for future inflation, nor do they take account of the time value of money received in the future.

Yields or returns on common stock are projections on the future. Free markets are continually evaluating financial circumstances: This translates into fluctuation in both principal and interest rates, which change, however infinitesimally, from hour to hour.

RISK FOR REWARDS

All investors, whether in stocks or bonds, have to continually weigh the various risks associated with their investments. Money in a savings account assumes no risk factor, since the return is precisely what was originally expected. The further the investment (for example, common stock) can potentially move away from the expected return, the greater the risk. In short, risk can be defined as deviation from certainty.

With the dozens of financial variables, from the health of the President to the level of housing starts, from the price of the dollar in foreign exchange to the Federal Reserve's discount rate, the major sources of risk can be reduced to three categories.

Interest Rate Risk

Since interest rates determine the price of borrowed money, their level has a vast impact on our society, which is now so heavily leveraged. (In 1980, 10 percent of the profit of the Fortune 500 companies went to servicing debt. Today, roughly 40 percent is dedicated to that purpose.) Budget deficits (plus off-budget borrowing, such as was necessary for the savings-and-loan crisis) require the federal government to borrow massive sums. The auction of Treasury paper to cover those deficits is perhaps the chief element in setting current rates, but other factors such as the discount and prime rates, plus fiscal and monetary moves, all have their effects. Interest rate changes are first felt in the bond market, and subsequently in the stock market.

There is a tipping point—generally thought to be about 10 percent for long bonds, or when the spread between stock yields and money market funds becomes excessive, say 7 or 8 percent—where the stock market can no longer compete with higher yields offered by the fixed-interest market. At that point, when prevailing interest rates become so high, money flows out of stocks and into bonds. The perception of higher inflation—and higher interest rates to compensate for it—suggests that stocks are definitely subject to interest rate risk.

Company Risk

If interest rate risk is first felt in the bond market, company or business risk is first appreciated in stocks. The risk, simply put, is that the company whose shares you have bought may go belly-up. While the bond holder has some recourse to the company's assets, the stockholder is left to the mercies of the exchange. Individual companies are open to the vagaries of the business cycle, government policies, product technology, management skills, labor relations, commodity shortages, hostile takeovers and natural calamities.

No two companies are affected in the same way, so company risk is sometimes called firm-specific risk or unsystematic risk, since what befalls one company does not usually have any bearing on another. Clearly, each company's vulnerability is somewhat different and in some ways contradictory. If you have a number of securities in a portfolio, the unsystematic risks will tend to cancel each other. A mutual fund of hundreds of companies has all but eliminated unsystematic risk, but almost the same relief can be obtained by individuals by diversifying their holdings with 10 or 15 securities. Since diversification can eliminate most company risk, this unsystematic risk is considered an unnecessary one to bear. In brief, prudent portfolio management requires canceling most company risk.

Market Risk

Forces that affect the whole economic system and bear directly on the markets are generally inescapable. Like the spring rain, they fall equally on all, and no amount of portfolio diversification reduces vulnerability. Some of the systemic risks are political and legislative, from new presidents and new tax codes; others are economic and financial, such as a recession or adjustments in currency value. Actions that affect all players are market risks, even though all participants may not be equally impacted. System-wide risk moves the stock market, as well as individual stocks, up and down.

The measure of this market volatility is termed *beta*, which equals unity, or 1. Specific securities can be measured against that general beta: They can be more volatile and have a beta of 1.5, or less volatile with a beta .5; the former is 50 percent more volatile than the market, while the latter is half as volatile as the general market. The beta evaluation (based on a mathematical formula) is a measurement of market or systematic risk.

There are other types of risks or uncertainties, such as future value of dollars or purchasing power risk, but the three—interest rate, company and market—are the ones of greatest concern for investors.

Managing Risk

To some degree, investors can manage risk, or at least make it tolerable. Each type of risk can be countered by employing some market tactic. This will assist in fine-tuning the amount of exposure that comes with each risk situation. For example, an investor can handle interest rate risk by appropriate timing to offset interest rate moves after careful study of the business cycle. An investor will try to lock in high yields if interest rates are about to fall (shortly before a recession commences) and, conversely, sell fixed-income securities if interest rates are about to rise (when business starts to accelerate dramatically).

In addition, derivative instruments such as bond futures can provide a hedge against unexpected trends. Such derivative debt instruments are more appropriate for the bondholder than the stock investor.

Market risk can be reduced, as noted earlier through diversification. Most investors make the mistake of buying only two or three issues. Economists have calculated that a portfolio of 12 to 15 different companies will eliminate 91 percent of all unsystematic or company risk. To eliminate the remaining business risk, you would have to buy hundreds of more companies. Since that is obviously impractical, it is perhaps wise to buy mutual funds until such time as your resources are ample enough to permit you to buy a dozen different issues.

Finally, market risk can be lowered by diversifying in time. By constantly investing in good times and in bad, when the market is high and when the market is low, it is possible to average your way to lower prices, or conversely increase your rate of return. Obviously, timing is a major concern to investors. There are two possible solutions to the problem of timing: Either develop the skills and talents necessary to trade the market, or side-step the problem altogether by using one of the formulas (to be explained later) for dollar averaging. The former will appeal to active traders, while the latter is attractive to long-term investors.

Risk versus Reward

Some investors assume that the riskiest investments return the highest rewards. That is not always the case. Part of the misunderstanding is due to the definition of what constitutes a risky investment—one person's risk is another's prudent action. Commodity contracts are considered the chanciest of investments (speculation, to be more precise), but they also have, on average, the worst record for rewarding speculation. Nine out of ten commodity trades show losses; it would, of course, be the other way around if the riskiest investments produced the highest rewards. Some speculators do indeed obtain dramatic rewards, but they are the exception.

It is possible to obtain higher returns (or the potential for greater rewards) when you take on more risk, but you may also obtain lower returns. The market pricing mechanism is not always efficient—and there are certainly periods of panic and euphoria when the pricing mechanism is out of whack—but over time, it adjusts the ratio of market price to expected return.

Stocks with volatile returns usually sell at lower market prices (say, less than $15) to compensate for the greater risk implicit in volatility. Stocks that are less risky and less volatile, more predictable in their rate of return, sell at higher prices (more than $15).

High-risk stocks do not necessarily outperform low-risk stocks in the long run. If they did produce higher yields, institutions with long investment horizons would pack their portfolios for long-term higher returns. They, along with individuals, would bid up the highly volatile issues, and as their price increased, their yields would fall to match that of the less volatile issues. In that case, the supposed high-risk stocks would only be more volatile.

Perhaps the reason risky stocks sell at lower prices to provide higher returns is that returns are not guaranteed. There is no guarantee that risky stocks will outperform less risky stocks, because what is expected doesn't always materialize. What can be observed is that in rising markets, high-risk stocks do better and provide better returns than lower-risk ones. But conversely they do worse—have lower returns—when the stock market is in retreat.

Thus there is no simple tradeoff between risk and reward—a portfolio of risky stocks is more likely to bring grief than gain. Some risky or volatile stocks in a portfolio might lift the normal return. However, even this accepted wisdom is challenged by Warren E. Buffett, the extraordinarily successful investor-chairman of Berkshire Hathaway (a single share of whose stock sells in the neighborhood of $8,000). Buffett is a proponent of value investing and suggests a negative correlation to risk-reward. He thinks that buying a more expensive stock (the definition of which is open to interpretation) is *more* risky than buying a cheaper stock. His analogy is simple: "If you buy a dollar bill for 60 cents, it's riskier than if you buy a dollar bill for 40 cents, but the expectation of reward is greater in the latter case. The greater the potential for reward in the value portfolio, the less risk there is."

What Is a "Safe" Investment?

The perception of risk also has much to do with the state of the financial markets. Bull markets diminish the awareness of risk. When prices rise, investors develop amnesia concerning caution. When prices are low, in the middle of a bear market, investors tend to be greatly concerned with risk and are overly cautious. The 1987 crash was a rude awakening, bringing the subject of risk center stage.

As investors slowly returned to the marketplace, avoidance of risk was uppermost in their minds. Subsequent market participation was in bonds, but also in the blue-chip sector, the Dow Jones Industrials. But there remained some dispute over where safety really lay—after all, it is contrary opinions that make for markets—and some serious, risk-averse investors avoided the blue-chip sector altogether.

Their reasoning illuminates some of the new crosscurrents that have entered the stock market in recent years. The bull market that started in the early 1980s was given impetus by computer-driven trading by large institutions. Not only were large blocks of stock traded based on predetermined programs, but core institutions and major market players started to use index arbitrage—the selling or buying of futures contracts based on an index or basket of stocks such as the Standard & Poor's 500 or 100—to profit from the inefficiencies or discrepancies in the futures and their underlying portfolios. Those program traders, along with portfolio insurance programs (another form of computer trading) to hedge exposure, gave the markets a great boost.

Conversely, they were disastrous on the downside and were held to be responsible by several postmortem investigations to be a major cause of meltdown Monday. Since computer-driven programs (some called them "mindless" or "no-news" investing techniques) made the market so risky or volatile, safety and prudence lay in avoiding blue-chip companies or stocks that were components of the major market indices. This led some investors to second-level and third-level equities—stocks they felt would be less risky and volatile, since they were not part of the indices and the computer programs.

IS THE MARKET EFFICIENT?

No doubt, some investors are risk-averse and attempt to realistically measure the riskiness and their potential return on investment. For the most part, they operate under the assumption that securities markets are efficient at measuring value. This "efficient market" theory has attracted a significant, but far from dominant, following on Wall Street and in academia. An efficient market is one in which all buyers and sellers trade on the basis of having access to full information concerning the securities in question. Or to put it another way, securities in an efficient market are priced on the basis of all known relevant facts.

In an efficient market, stock prices will fluctuate around a consensus value until news or developments move the consensus to some other value. This wandering price movement is called a *random walk*. Without a reason to move, this randomness continues. Since all significant information is already in the price of the security, additional analysis is virtually meaningless.

Believers in the random walk in an efficient market see no value in trying to ascertain trends or predict direction. It is pointless, in their estimation, to believe that experience, insight or simple intuitive market smarts can be profitable. In short, if investors are averse to risk and markets are efficient, there is no point in attempting to outguess other investors, and rational portfolios will be risk-free. One might as well use the dart-board approach to investing, since the results of throwing darts at stock tables will do no worse or no better than any other selection technique.

The random walk does not appeal to many investors and professional money managers, since they believe the markets are not always efficient. Indeed, there are long periods when the markets are overpriced or underpriced because of excessive optimism or dire pessimism. (For example, from

August 1982 to June 1983 stocks rose by about 65 percent, but the year before, they fell 25 percent.) These investors and money managers sense that they can take advantage of these disjunctures. Moreover, while information is indeed the lifeblood of markets, it is possible to generate greater insights and more knowledgeable analyses on a private basis. Public knowledge is not a substitute for private wisdom, experience and analytical skills.

Nevertheless, some investors and money mangers are convinced of the efficient market theory's merits. They do not believe that they can turn in a superior performance in trading a portfolio of securities. Therefore, they concentrate on buying companies with superior management.

The business managers and owners (in the better companies) are trying to maximize profits, attempting to make the company as successful as possible. They are surrogates for the buyers/owners of the company shares. Not only are they out to provide the most profitable performance that the company is capable of, but if left to their own devices they insulate the stock investor from the inevitable fear and greed that is a psychological companion to investing. If you follow the efficient market theory, once you have chosen the best companies in a diversified universe, you do not believe in frequent buying and selling; as an individual, you are not likely to be more capable, wiser or more astute than the people who run the company. Constant trading, hence, is a costly and probably unsuccessful indulgence.

GET TO KNOW YOUR INVESTMENT PERSONALITY

How you look at the stock market is as important as knowing your risk tolerance.

If you are convinced that the stock market is nothing but a crapshoot, that investing in it is a gamble or that it is manipulated by large institutions to the detriment of small and individual investors, you had better rethink your involvement. If you operate from any of those premises, you are likely to come to grief: You will buy (or sell) on rumors, tips and gossip; you will attribute your successes (or failures) to pure chance or to the unknown actions of others. In short, you will be playing a loser's game, since inevitably either your luck will run out or you will be the last to hear the "inside" information from the institutions.

Nor should you be an individual investor if you cannot tolerate the inherent fluctuations of security prices. As stock averages climb, there will be upside explosions and downside corrections that send prices reeling. The percentage changes may be the same as a decade earlier, but the abstract numbers are now greater. Fear of volatility will lead you to act inappropriately—to your detriment.

Some private investors and institutions have come to the conclusion that they either cannot outperform the general market (and have no wish to attempt it) or are wary of too much volatility. They have chosen to invest in index funds, mutual funds that mimic the broad averages. These funds particularly appeal to money managers who are frequently judged on their performance vis-a-vis the averages.

If you wish to participate in an investment program but are suspicious of how markets operate or cannot tolerate rapid fluctuations, then either an index fund or some other form of mutual fund will relieve you of both consternations.

This book is written from the point of view that financial markets are human institutions and that they are largely rational. This does not necessarily mean that they are always efficient, work smoothly or foretell the future with great precision. Markets are more than simple mechanisms.

They respond to the human emotions of hope, despair, fear, greed, uncertainty and euphoria.

Most investors do not follow the dictates of the random walk theory, that direction of the market or individual stocks cannot be predicted on the basis of past information, for a number of reasons. Whether it be pride, competitiveness or a desire to excel, it is clear that they wish to be in charge of their investment activity. There is a strong desire to match objectives with risk tolerance. Even if monkeys throwing darts could approximate the same return on investment, it would be bizarre to put them in charge of your money. Most investors believe that markets are logical and respond to knowledge. What is needed is more information and better analysis, rather than a belief that further information is useless and prediction pointless.

This book is dedicated to the principles that discipline, caution and hard work, plus a smattering of insight and common sense will allow you to operate profitably in today's business and economic environment. There are no guarantees, but a solid investment program has historically more than kept abreast of inflation and has doubled the rate of return on invested funds over simple savings plans. If you are concerned with maintaining the value of your assets now and in the foreseeable future, the following information and tools should prove exceedingly helpful.

Y · O · U · R   M · O · V · E

- Determine whether you have adequate savings before starting an investment program. You should have at least $10,000 to $20,000 in short-term and long-term savings.

- Measure your comfort level. What kind of risks are you prepared to take and with what proportion of your funds?
- Consider the three types of risk present in the stock market. Take steps to balance the risks and counter or hedge their potential impacts.
- Choose your level of activity. If you believe in the efficient market theory, pick the best companies and be prepared to live with market ups and downs. If you believe that markets are sometimes efficient and sometimes not, closely monitor market activity to take advantage of fluctuations, inefficiencies and disjunctures.

• 2 •

Can You Beat the Market?

A MATTER OF CYCLES

Can you make money in the stock market? The un-equivocal answer is yes! But if you ask whether you can outpace the general averages, then the answer must be hedged: perhaps. In some years you may, but in some years you may not. The average investor really has no need to be concerned about how the Dow Jones Industrial Average or the Standard & Poor's 500 is performing. The immediate and pressing question is, How is your own portfolio growing or holding up? Are you exceeding the rate of return you could have if you simply left your money in a savings account or U.S. Savings Bond over a period of years? If not, you had either better exit from the stock market, hire a professional or attempt to understand what you are doing wrong in order to improve your performance.

Before attempting to beat the market or, at the very least, improve your chances and your performance, you should try to understand not only what the markets have done in the past, but what moves they traditionally make through the course of a normal business cycle. Economic cycles are as old as the Bible. Whether it was the ancient seven years of feast and famine or just the last business boom, which started in 1982 (only to be temporarily interrupted by the October 1987 crash) and lasted until the start of the 1990 recession, there is a noticeable repetition in the ups and downs of business.

The business cycle, from boom to bust, consists of five stages of economic activity: revival, expansion, maturation, contraction and finally recession. While the duration of the cycle might be seven years, it is more likely to last between three and five years. Before 1929, the average recession in this century lasted 21 months; since 1933, the average has been only 11 months. There is no telling how long each stage will last, and the agency that determines when the cycle is over and a recession has commenced, the National Bureau of Economic Research, does so from a position of hindsight.

Why is it important for the investor to understand the trajectory of the business cycle? To the investor, the stages are somewhat like the nightly stars to the navigator: They indicate direction and speed. The road signs are the various statistical indicators compiled by the Commerce Department. They fall into three groups: leading, coincident, and lagging indicators. Each category has a dozen or so components. Investors also eagerly await many other pieces of economic information—money supply, interest rates and trade figures, among others—depending on the economic situation. For example, if trade balances are critical, those figures will receive an inordinate amount of attention. The leading indicators, however, hold constant interest for investors since they are made up of predictive measurements. The components of the leading indicators index are shown in Figure 2.1.

Rough correlations can be made between the business cycles and the movements of stock prices, though at times they can be ambiguous if not downright deceptive. The important consideration for investors to remember is that the securities markets—whether stocks, bonds or commodities—are anticipatory mechanisms. Even when the markets are perfectly efficient as to what is known or knowable,

FIGURE 2.1   The Components of the Leading Indicators Index

1. Average workweek hours of manufacturing

2. Average weekly initial unemployment insurance claims

3. Manufacturers' new orders for consumer goods and materials

4. S&P 500 composite index

5. Plant and equipment orders and contracts

6. Index of new private housing authorized by permit

7. Supplier delivery sub-component of the purchasing managers' index

8. University of Michigan index of consumer expectations

9. Net change in inventories on hand and on order

10. Change in sensitive materials price

11. Money supply: M2

they are already anticipating actions and reactions days or months in the future. Therefore, the correlations are always inexact, since future perceptions are at variance with each other.

Revival

Generally speaking, a revival of the economy, the first stage, will show a number of positive indicators. To put it the other way around, you can tell the economy is in the early stages of a revival when the gross national product begins to expand after negative or flat growth, employment expands, hours worked increases, initial unemployment claims level off and start to fall, capital spending starts to increase, production of consumer durable products rises and government spending picks up, since there are more earnings to tax. In brief, a revived economy shows a determined sense of euphoria after months, or sometimes years, of recession and downbeat predictions.

There also are a number of monetary indicators that herald a revival. In the contraction and recession stages, the government stops worrying about an overheated economy and inflation. The Federal Reserve Board looks to ways of stimulating business. It will cut the discount rate (the interest rates it charges member banks who borrow from it) a number of times; it will increase the money supply targets and push the federal funds rate down. As the revival starts in earnest, the Fed will probably overshoot its money supply targets.

What does a revival stage mean for stock investors? Obviously, it is time to buy stock to participate in the economy's expansion, and especially to profit from a selected portfolio of companies that will partake in the next boom. (Each boom follows the same cyclicality of events, but the nature or characteristics may well be different: some emphasize high technology, others basic industrial goods. More on this in the chapter on stock selection.)

Investors who monitor the business cycle will not wait for the revival. They will anticipate it. They will have started to accumulate their shares while the market is in the doldrums and prices are depressed. The same is true for bonds: Prices may be down, as interest rates tend to peak early in a recession. It is against human nature, of course, to buy securities in periods of gloom. But it is precisely in those times when risk is lowest when, to repeat the words of Warren Buffett, you can buy a dollar for 40 cents. Companies that you might consider fall into the blue-chip category—household names that investors can easily identify and feel comfortable with. They are likely to be consumer types of companies, such as Woolworth and McDonald's, that are widely recognized. Since interest rates have dropped, interest-sensitive businesses such as utilities and telephone companies should also be considered.

Extensive study by the National Bureau of Economic Research found that stock prices tended to lead business cycle changes by four months. Thus if you are going to use the business cycle to forecast stock prices, you must be aware that the anticipatory nature of markets shows that stock prices start to move up before the cycle apparently changes.

Expansion

The next stage of the business cycle after the revival, expansion, is also a generally good time to buy common stock. Inflation has started to pick up, and one should invest in companies that are not adversely affected by higher interest rates. Capital goods now show a revival, and companies in appliances, automobiles, furniture, home furnishings, houses and machine tools have full order books.

Maturation

The subsequent stage after expansion is maturation. This transition can be identified by a number of business cycle developments: Business is spending heavily on basic industry and new plants, since everyone in the business community is now convinced that the good times are permanent. Overbuilding is one sure sign of a top. Another sign is capacity utilization. When 85 percent or more of the industrial capacity is in use, the economy is in the last stages of maturation. Labor supplies are tight, but hours worked have leveled off. Consumers start to hold back on the purchase of durable items and housing starts start to turn down. It is time to leave consumer-oriented companies.

On the monetary front, the Fed starts to lean against the wind and raises the discount rate and the federal funds rate. Monetary targets are lowered and the monetary base contracts. When these signs become unmistakable, it is time either to sell stocks, sell stocks short, and/or move to defensive issues that will ride out the next stage, the contraction. Traditionally, defensive issues are food, tobacco, beverage and brewery companies.

Contraction and Recession

Contractions and recessions are perhaps more easily identified than other stages of the business cycle. At first, the horizon clouds and then the squalls start. Gloom and doom pervade the general atmosphere. Stories about plant closings, the industrial sector losing its competitive edges, insurmountable foreign suppliers, falling wage rates and increased unemployment claims are all on the front page. At first the stories are sporadic, but as the contraction moves to recession, they begin to flood the media. Slowly, everyone is convinced that times will never get better. Interest rates come down. The Federal Reserve tries to stop the economic slump by cutting the discount rate, lowering the federal funds rate, but increasing the money supply.

The Fed's Influence on Business Cycles

The business cycle is an event that no one controls, but one which central banks around the world and the Fed in the United States try to modify and ameliorate. Their success in manipulating economies is difficult to gauge, especially since global markets and international agreements often contradict or diminish a central bank's activities. The Fed has a history of overshooting its mark and inevitably creating too much of a good thing.

For example, in the spring and summer of 1987, the Fed moved to support the weakening price of the dollar in the foreign exchange markets by increasing interest rates, a fact many observers think helped to trigger the October meltdown. A day after the crash, the Fed changed gears abruptly and flooded the system with liquidity. It was as if the business cycle had moved through a recession in two days and the Fed was in an accommodating position: Supporting the financial system and the economy became a priority, rather than supporting the dollar.

The Fed's reversal in October was intended to reduce panic, a singular occurrence. Generally, the Fed creates a boom in the cycle by lowering rates and injecting money into the economy. This tends to stimulate investment at the expense of consumption, and businesses look more profitable than they otherwise might be. As normal market forces exert themselves against the Fed's manipulation, the public keeps borrowing instead saving because of the low rates, and soon demand starts to push interest rates up. This would throttle business, so the Fed pumps even more money into the system and inflation appears in the maturation stage. When the Fed can no longer follow that course, it tightens the money supply and the stock market takes a header as liquidity is drained from the system.

Fed tightening is a sign for you as an investor to turn cautious and consider selling some, or indeed all, of your portfolio, depending on your time frame and the tax implications. Clearly, heirloom holdings need not be disturbed because of fluctuations in a business cycle. Nor may you wish to incur a tax liability because of a temporary recession.

The business cycle and the stock market move loosely in tandem. If one could anticipate the business cycle, predicting market moves would be easier. Unfortunately, everyone has 20/20 hindsight, but few are gifted with perfect foresight. What makes it more difficult of late is the modification of the cycle as a result of new trends and changes in the economy. Geoffrey Moore, director of Columbia University's Center for International Business Cycle Research, notes that contemporary business cycles are shorter and milder and thus harder to identify. Moreover, the rise of the service economy has altered some of the cycle's characteristics. Service businesses, now responsible for a majority of business activity, are more stable: They have no inventory to work off while the plant suspends operations and thus provide no cause for a classic inventory recession with all its attendant ripples.

In addition, the government is now hyperactive in intervening when the economy is in trouble: not only the Fed, but Congress and executive agencies. The result is an attempt to modify the swings of the business cycle. It is not clear, however, that government action always produces the desired consequence: in 1981 it was government action against high interest rates that brought about the worst recession since World War II.

IT'S ALL IN THE TIMING

The business cycle can be a guide to market forces, but it does not provide a tactical strategy for stock selection. Clearly, the market price of some securities is tied to the business cycle—these will be discussed more fully in the chapter on stock selection. However, by investing with, rather than ignoring, the business cycle, you are likely to improve your chances for success. (*Contrarian* investors

FIGURE 2.2   Chart of Leading Indicators, Plotted Monthly
(shaded areas indicate recession)

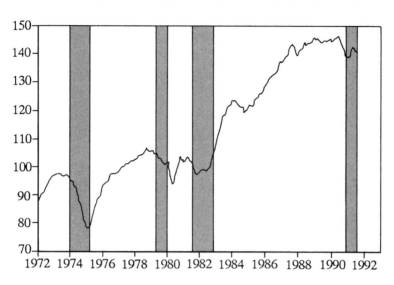

SOURCE: Adapted from the U.S. Department of Commerce.

do not ignore the business cycle, but use it for their own
particular reasons.) Some of the greatest advances in stock
indices took place concurrently with advancing or expan-
sionary business cycles. Look at the last cycle: Business
picked up late in 1982, emerging from a recession in
December; the bull market in stocks had started just a few
months earlier, in August 1982. Conversely, most of the
recessions since 1970 have been accompanied by market
retreats: 1973–74, 1979–80, 1981–82 and 1990–91.

Evidently, it pays to invest in the context of a business
cycle. The business cycle, though, is different each time it
occurs, and sometimes the leading indicators do not lead.
(See Figure 2.2.) Investors looking for a timing mechanism
to tell them when to enter and when to leave the stock market cannot rely on one indicator to foretell the progression

of a business cycle, but must also understand the implications of economic policy, political developments and international agreements, along with the outlook for interest rates and corporate profits.

Timing your investments from the perspective of the business cycle may well increase your likelihood of success, but this approach poses one serious, perhaps insurmountable problem for some investors: It requires buying securities in a recession, when the outlook is truly depressing and when everyone is convinced that this time the markets will never recover, that the dollar is on an irreversible slide, that foreign competitors will eat our lunch and that American profitability is part of past history.

Conversely, it also requires selling securities when the rosy scenario is in the limelight: Profits are bounding ahead, the economy has never been stronger, the dollar is ascendant and foreign competition is easy to defeat. In short, one must act contrary to one's psychological perceptions and common sense; doing this not easy and is rarely comfortable. But it is precisely this contrarian approach that lowers your risk on the downside and increases your profit on the upside.

By buying common stock when no one else wants to, you are likely to be purchasing shares at or near their lows. The sellers have beaten down the price, since they have unloaded their holdings in the past few weeks or months. Your risk of a further major move downward is small. To cite an old Wall Street maxim, "Airplanes don't crash when they are on the ground."

It is difficult for you to sell your shares when markets are rising, but that is exactly the time that shares are in demand, when other investors are willing to step up to higher prices. You may not realize the top price—almost no one does—but you do obtain a capital gain. As another old Wall Street clichè has it, you never go broke taking a profit.

Consequently, the difficulties in attempting to invest on the basis of business cycle signals are multiple: The booms and busts are less pronounced than in former years, the leading indicators are sometimes confusing and out of sync and even the acquisitive nature of investors makes it hard to buy when gloom prevails and sell when everyone is euphoric. Nevertheless, it has been one of the most profitable methods of investing for anyone concerned about timing entry and exit points. There are other methods, which shall be discussed later, that ignore timing: Some averaging techniques can be highly successful.

JUST HOW SUCCESSFUL ARE THE PROFESSIONALS?

As indicated earlier, as an investor, you should be concerned with your own objectives, rather than with what other investors are doing. Professional money managers may be evaluated on the basis of their performance records, but bear in mind that their goals may not be the same as yours. Just as the S&P 500 average is an indication of what an unmanaged cross section of publicly traded securities are doing, the average activities of professional managers illustrate the other extreme—the results of specifically targeted objectives. Clearly, some professionals do extraordinarily well. However, individual investors can take much comfort in the fact that they can succeed without the aid of money managers.

In 1986, a sample of 322 investment advisers had an average gain of 17.4 percent, compared with a gain of 18.6 percent for the S&P 500 stock index. Over a ten-year period starting in 1977, the median equity fund earned 14.0 percent per year, compared to the S&P 500's average of 13.8 percent per year. The findings are consistent with most reports on portfolio performance. In the last five years, the S&P 500 outperformed fully three-quarters of all equity funds. Or to put it another way, while there are indeed some exceedingly successful professional money managers, on average they tend to underperform the market. And sometimes the charge to investors for this underperformance—a sales charge of 4.0 to 8.5 percent, the 12b-1 distribution fees, and the management expenses—can be considerable.

In brief, private individuals can and do outperform institutions on a regular basis as a result of their own intelligence and initiative. Numerous case histories are cited in the *Journal of the American Association of Individual Investors*. Institutions frequently perform poorly, or no better than the general averages, simply because they are often so large that regardless of their purpose, their component companies reflect market activity. It is rare for a fund with 100, 300 or 500 companies to be anything but a surrogate for the market. Moreover, funds must skip smaller and often unlisted companies, since their massive size would adversely affect market price. Individual investors have a special advantage because of their size—it is an advantage that should not be overlooked.

CONTRARIAN INVESTING

The classic approach to investing—in tandem with the business cycle—is meant to take advantage of the patterns that have long been realized by investment professionals. In practice, it requires anticipating the cycles to be truly successful. Most investors tend to buy when others are buying, and vice versa. This tendency to crowd together does not necessarily make most investors wrong. However, one school of thought, which has attracted a number of convinced followers, is certain (in its extreme form) that most of the populace is wrong most of the time. A more refined version of this theme states that when everyone thinks alike, everyone is likely to be wrong. This somewhat elitist view has a long and honorable history based on the manias and fantasies that visit mankind with intermittent regularity. Greed breeds gullibility.

People have put money in the most bizarre inventions—square cannon balls, pills that turn water into gasoline—and occasionally have been conned out of substantial sums by investing in salted gold mines and property below the low-water mark. Nothing remarkable about that. When, however, whole populaces bid the price of tulips in 17th-century Holland to astronomical heights or when Englishmen in the 18th century wildly scrambled to buy shares of the South Sea Company because of its harebrained scheme to exchange the national debt for shares of the company's skyrocketing stock—then one is witnessing mass hysteria. Nor is it a past phenomena: In 1980, gold was bid up to $875 per ounce and silver to $50 per ounce. When they are not being manipulated by individuals, markets on occasion get carried away in a trance of group hypnosis.

The first compilation of mass hysteria (and a source book of contrary opinion) was *Extraordinary Popular Delusions and the Madness of Crowds*, written by Charles MacKay, in 1841. This was followed by *The Crowd*, a study on social psychology written by Gustave Le Bon in 1895. Contrary thinking received its first modern formulation *The Art of Contrary Thinking*, by Humphrey B. Neill (1954). The common thread in all these books is that crowd psychology causes extreme madness of booms and busts; as individuals, men and woman are rational but succumb to destabilizing emotion when acting in unison. The latest exponent of contrarian thinking is David N. Dreman, who is convinced that investors do not learn from past mistakes. He is convinced that circumstances do really seem very different each time, although in fact each set of circumstances was remarkably similar to the last. Dreman is the head of a successful Wall Street management company.

Contrarians use extreme crowd behavior as a guide to investing, since overwhelming consensus forecasts are frequently wrong. Inevitably, there remains a whole host of important but unknowable factors that cause the trend to change, and usually abruptly. As the famous biologist Rene Dubos remarked, "Present trends never continue." Moreover, what is generally expected rarely occurs because of the feedback factor. This principle, well known to engineers, states that the factors that produce a result are themselves modified, altered, strengthened or weakened in an uncontrolled fashion by that result.

Investors act in anticipation of market direction, thereby changing the course of the market. When an overwhelming consensus has developed, most investors have already done what they are going to do. There is little strength or momentum left to keep advancing or retreating; all the buying power is used up, or all the selling has crested. Contrarians suggest that to succeed, investors must be disciplined and hard-headed, not swayed by popular sentiment. This is particularly difficult, since it is so unnatural—people are social beings and natural joiners. When stocks are generally in the news and are widely touted by magazines and brokers, investors are drawn to them—everyone wishes to own them. As they are bid up in price, a buying frenzy takes place until some disappointing news or earnings sends the stock crashing down as the earliest investors leave the market.

Contrarians avoid consensus movements, whether in market direction or in individual stocks. They look for neglected issues, companies that security analysts do not follow, and companies that are mundane and unexciting—pedestrian companies that to contrarians typically represent forgotten industries, such as paint, furniture, metal containers, fasteners, funeral services and farm machinery, to name but a few.

Contrarians find their best values in extreme markets. It is not enough to find a majority view and then disagree with it. Majorities, after all, have been known to be right. Here is Neill's response to the question, Is the public wrong all the time?

> The answer is, decidedly, "no." The public is per-haps right more of the time than not. In stock-mar-ket parlance, the public is right during the trends but wrong at both ends.

> One can assert that the public is usually wrong at junctures of events and at terminals of trends.

> So to be cynical, you might say, "Yes, the public is always wrong when *it pays to be right*—but is far from wrong in the meantime.

Neill raises another important point, one which con-trarians and other investors should consider at length in a media-oriented environment. Without subscribing to a con-spiracy theory, it must be acknowledged that the forces conditioning the public's thinking and perceptions, espe-cially the government, are indeed powerful. In his book, *It Pays To Be Contrary*, Neill observes that:

> ... errors and faulty forecasts are more likely under a managed economy than under a so-called laissez-faire system of society. . . . Under a managed sys-tem of society, into which we are steadily becoming more deeply involved, propaganda becomes an ever more powerful tool of the "managers." . . . How to separate propaganda from actual news takes a keen mind familiar with news-gathering and propaganda agencies. But it does not take a keen mind to esti-

mate public opinion—and business opinions—and then to sit down and analyze opposing viewpoints.

Recent stock market fads have occasionally gone to extremes, such as was the case in casino stocks, companies that manufactured drugs for growing hair and for birth control and Japanese securities. Contrarians certainly have ample examples to illustrate their thesis.

Contrarians are obliged to take the long view and be willing to live with the sense that they are always in a minority. There are some "sentiment" indicators that help orient any investor who finds this attitude accommodating. For the broad market there are two published indicators: *Investors Intelligence* publishes a weekly poll of investment advisers who are bullish, bearish or in the correction camp (basically bullish but expect short-term weakness); *MarketVane* publishes a weekly poll of futures-trading advisers to determine the bullish consensus. Contrarians use these polls as markers—high bullish readings are signs of market tops, and conversely low ones are indicative of market bottoms.

Other indicators of investor sentiment are listed in *Investor's Business Daily* in a table of measurements that offer guidance in determining active investor attitudes (Figure 2.3).

The contrarian approach has much value, in that it imbues investors with a healthy dose of skepticism about trends and market prices. The trend is not your friend, according to a common observation among some technical analysts. And high market prices are sometimes the result of excessive optimism. But it is quite a leap to believe, as many contrarians do, that market prices are wrong because of emotional excess and crowd psychology.

Panics have indeed occurred on occasion, but these have been mercifully rare. The investor is perhaps best advised to step aside from the runaway locomotive rather

FIGURE 2.3 Psychological Market Indicators

PSYCHOLOGICAL MARKET INDICATORS	Current	5 YEAR				12 MONTH			
		High	Date	Low	Date	High	Date	Low	Date
1. % Investment Advisers Bearish (50% = Bullish; 20% = Bearish) % Invest. Advisers Bullish (35% Bullish; 55% Bearish), – Investor's Intelligence	28.9% 51.8%	57.3% 64.4%	(2/20/90) (1/27/87)	11.8% 21.1%	(2/24/87) (12/5/88)	56.0% 58.6%	(9/11/90) (3/4/91)	23.1% 27.9%	(4/29/91) (9/24/90)
2. Odd Lot Short Sales/Odd Lot Sales	0.344%	36.1%	(9/15/86)	0.04%	(9/11/87)	31.1%	(9/14/90)	0.34%	(9/9/91)
3. Public/NYSE Specialist Short Sales (above 0.6 Bullish; below 0.35 Bearish)	0.57	1.45	(10/12/90)	0.31	(10/23/87)	1.45	(10/12/90)	0.50	(5/31/91)
4. Short Interest Ratio (NYSE Short Interest/Avg. Daily Volume prior 30 days)	4.29	5.81	(1/16/91)	1.67	(2/17/87)	5.81	(1/16/91)	3.57	(3/8/91)
5. Ratio of price premiums on Puts versus Calls	0.68	1.74	(2/11/91)	0.03	(10/19/87)	1.74	(2/11/91)	0.27	(9/24/90)
6. Ratio of Trading Volume in Puts versus Calls	0.81	1.07	(9/21/90)	0.26	(10/21/87)	1.07	(9/21/90)	0.40	(4/23/91)
7. Mutual Fund Share Purchases/Redemptions (X – Money Market Funds)	2.14	3.64	(1/1/87)	0.63	(10/30/87)	2.14	(7/31/91)	1.32	(10/31/90)
8. AMEX Daily Trading Volume as % of NYSE Daily Volume	8.13%	15.1%	(12/1/88)	2.56%	(6/17/88)	13.2%	(12/31/90)	4.84%	(1/22/91)
9. OTC Daily Trading Volume as % of NYSE Daily Volume	102%	143%	(5/20/88)	35.6%	(12/9/87)	122%	(3/28/91)	61.1%	(1/18/91)
10. Number of Stock Splits in INVESTOR'S DAILY INDEX (prior 30 days)	48	169	(6/11/87)	20	(11/26/90)	75	(7/9/91)	20	(11/26/90)
11. New issues in Last Year as % of All Stocks on NYSE	12.7%	49.5%	(3/5/87)	9.20%	(5/2/91)	15.2%	(9/20/90)	9.20%	(5/2/91)
12. Price – to – Book Value of Dow Jones Industrial Average	2.72	4.37	(8/25/87)	2.07	(5/23/88)	2.81	(8/29/91)	2.07	(10/11/90)
13. Price to Earnings Ratio of Dow Jones Industrial Average	18.8	21.0	(10/6/87)	9.79	(11/16/88)	19.3	(8/23/91)	11.2	(10/11/90)
14. Current Dividend Yield of Dow Jones Industrial Average	3.14%	4.29%	(10/11/90)	2.58%	(8/25/87)	4.29%	(10/11/90)	3.06%	(8/29/91)

SOURCE: Reprinted by permission of *INVESTOR'S DAILY, America's Business Newspaper* (Sept. 10, 1991).
© INVESTOR'S DAILY, INC., 1991

than attribute profound meaning to its erratic action. Contrarians believe that most investors are always overreacting—a dubious assumption at best and one without much evidence.

Y·O·U·R   M·O·V·E

- Position yourself to take advantage of the most important friend an investor has—the business cycle. If you can manage to be in the stock market when a business boom commences (and out of it when a recession looms), a rising tide will lift most seaworthy boats.
- Be careful not to rely on only one financial indicator. Select half a dozen that have proven trustworthy in the past to determine what stage the business cycle is currently passing through.
- Pay special attention to the actions of the Fed. If interest rates start to escalate, be wary of tight credit and its effect on the stock market. The old rule of thumb of three steps and a stumble remains a valid early warning signal of lower stock prices.
- If you choose to use the services of a professional money manager make sure you select one who has a long and positive track record. Check with individuals and published results from a mutual fund for documentation.
- Be cautious in joining mass movements or investing in "sure things." Contrary thinking can be helpful, especially at important turns in the stock market. Investing solely on contrary indicators can be dangerous, not to mention lonely.
- Follow published sentiment indicators and try to stay with the prevalent psychological tone of the market.

• 3 •

How To Pick Stocks

THE FUNDAMENTALS

Security analysis begins with an understanding of the businesses or companies you are considering. Most investors, whether amateur or professional, feel obliged to know the fundamentals about a company they plan to invest in, both to satisfy their curiosity and to act responsibly. The fundamentals encompass a number of items, from product lines, tendered services, management experience, labor relations, industry stability, political sensitivity, demographic vulnerability and a whole host of financial facts and ratios. Fundamental analysis is based on the sound theory that you can never know enough about a given situation—that the more information you have, the fewer unpleasant surprises you will face.

Not every analyst is impressed with this fundamental approach to security analysis and the evaluation of stock prices. Technical analysis is based on other considerations than the fundamentals of the company or industry. Since information is certainly nice to know, it is nevertheless always insufficient in the view of technicians. It is better not to be confused with what is, after all, sometimes confusing, contradictory and complex data. No one ever gives completely satisfactory answers as to why prices move on fundamental information.

Technicians are essentially interested in the action of market prices, whether taken individually or in a group, whether for a day, a month or a year. Price movements through a period of time graphically reveal the simplest and most direct law of economics—supply and demand. Alexander Pope remarked that "the proper study of mankind is man," and technicians likewise believe that the proper study of security valuation is price action. John Magee, the father of modern technical security analysis, was totally isolated from fundamental information. His professional life was rather like Marcel Proust, the author of *Remembrance of Things Past*, who wrote in a windowless, cork-lined room so that he too could be isolated from fundamental sensate experience. (Magee's work, *Technical Analysis of Stock Trends*, is the bible of technicians.)

Today, technical analysis is no longer considered a subterranean strategy, a tool of a handful of isolated clerks. Technicians are now welcome in the front office, and technical analysis is viewed as a complement to fundamental analysis rather than an opposing and suspect ideology. In brief, technical analysis has achieved recognition and respect in spite of the fact that efficient-market theorists and random walkers have attacked some of the basic premises of technical analysis. No doubt, modern computer techniques and the popularization of computer graphics have done much to enhance the value of technical analysis. The following analysis of security prices will review both fundamental and technical approaches in order to improve your sense of market timing.

HOW TO READ THE ANNUAL REPORT

The purpose of analysis is to determine whether a security is overpriced, underpriced or priced in line with its market value. You need this information if you are to make a reasonable and rational forecast about the future of the company and the future price of the stock. Only by examining the so-called "financials," the basic summary documents of the business, can you make that determination.

The financials an investor must consult can be reduced to three documents: the balance sheet, the income statement and the summary of changes in the company's financial position. These primary documents are found in the annual report (a more complete version is known as the 10K report and is filed with the Securities and Exchange Commission), which can be obtained directly from the company or through a brokerage house. Concise summaries can be located in secondary sources such as *Standard & Poor's Stock Guide and Stock Reports, Value Line's Investment Survey, Moody's Industrial Manual, Media General's Financial Services* and *Dow Jones News Retrieval Service*, among other hard-copy and electronic data base sources.

The Balance Sheet

This document is considered most important to investors, since it reveals the financial condition of the company. Income may fluctuate from quarter to quarter and from year to year; therefore, it is imperative to know about the underlying health and resources as documented by the balance sheet. Naturally, a series of annual balance sheets from the end of successful fiscal years makes comparisons and trends apparent.

The balance sheet (Table 3.1) is derived from a basic principle discovered during the Italian Renaissance—single-entry accounting. To be in order, an accounting has to balance with equal offsetting expenses (payables) and income (receivables). Thus one side of a balance sheet, the

TABLE 3.1 Typical Consolidated Balance Sheet
High Tech Tools, Inc. (in thousands)

		June 30, 1988	June 30, 1989
Assets			
Current Assets:			
(1)	Cash and equivalents	$ 5,000	$ 4,000
(2)	Marketable securities, short-term investments	1,500	1,000
(3)	Accounts receivable	3,000	2,500
(4)	Inventories	7,500	6,000
(5)	Prepaid expenses	500	350
	Total Current Assets	$17,500	$13,850
Fixed Assets:			
(6)	Property, plant, equipment	$ 8,000	$ 6,500
Intangible Assets:			
(7)	Licenses	$ 1,250	$850
(8)	Goodwill	600	550
	Total Fixed/Intangible Assets	$ 9,850	$ 7,900
	Total Assets	$27,350	$21,750
Liabilities and Stockholders' Equity			
Current Liabilities:			
(9)	Accounts payable	$ 7,500	$ 6,000
(10)	Notes and obligations	350	300
(11)	Accrued expenses	75	65
(12)	Taxes owed	120	85
	Total Current Liabilities	$ 8,045	$ 6,450
Long-Term Liabilities:			
(13)	Bonds debts due after one year	$ 7,500	$ 7,250
	Total Liabilities	$15,545	$13,700
Stockholder's Equity:			
(14)	Preferred stock	$ 1,000	$ 1,000
(15)	Common stock	5,000	5,000
(16)	Additional paid-in capital	150	150
(17)	Retained earnings	22,500	21,000
(18)	**Total Stockholders' Equity**	$28,650	$27,150
(19)	**Total Liabilities and Stockholders' Equity**	**$44,195**	**$40,850**

assets, must equal the other side, the liabilities, plus capital (or stockholders' equity). The basic equation is:

$$\text{Assets} = \text{Liabilities} + \text{Capital}$$

From the point of view of stockholders it is:

$$\text{Capital} = \text{Assets} - \text{Liabilities}$$

What the company owns, minus what it owes, belongs to the shareholders or owners.

What the company owns can be summarized under three headings:

- *Current assets:* cash and equivalent, marketable securities, accounts receivable (monies due the company), inventory (the value of finished goods, work in progress and raw materials); prepaid expenses
- *Fixed assets:* plant and equipment, real estate
- *Intangible assets*: licenses, trademarks, copyrights, goodwill

The sum of these three groups of assets is equal to total assets.

What the company is owed, plus the capital, is noted under liabilities and stockholders' equity:

- *Current liabilities*: accounts payable (monies owed), notes and obligations due within one year, accrued expenses, taxes owed
- *Long-term liabilities*: bonds and debts due after one year
- *Deferred taxes*
- *Stockholders' equity*: the value of securities issued (common and preferred) and outstanding, additional paid-in capital, retained earnings

Thus the balance sheet is a snapshot on a particular date of what the company possesses, what its debts and obligations are, and finally its net worth. Stockholders' equity is contingent on the validity of the underlying figures. There are different ways to arrive at the value of inventory or the valuation of plant and equipment. Is the real estate reported at cost on the day it was purchased or when it was last appraised for tax purposes or at current market value? Companies, and their auditors, have some discretion within generally accepted accounting practices.

It is up to the investor to read the footnotes, refer to secondary sources and finally ask management for clarification. Conservative companies will tend to understate the value of their assets, while aggressive ones are likely to overvalue them and give undue weight to intangibles, such as the value of trademarks and goodwill. The purpose of the balance sheet is to reveal, not conceal, but the latter is sometimes the case.

The Income Statement

The income statement, or profit-and-loss statement, is almost as important as the balance sheet. If the balance sheet is a snapshot, the income statement is a movie or videocassette, since it attempts to portray an image over time (Table 3.2). The statement starts with the business's revenues and, after accounting for expenses, ends with the earnings per share of common stock. Revenues, or sales, is the most significant source of income for most companies. But it is not the only source, especially among holding companies, financial organizations, banks and firms that receive substantial funds from dividends, the sale of assets or income from investment. Operating revenue and other sources of income will be listed and should be considered in appreciating the business's progress.

TABLE 3.2 Typical Consolidated Statement of Income
High Tech Tools, Inc. (in thousands)

	June 30, 1989	June 30, 1988	June 30, 1987
(1) Revenues	$32,500	$27,125	$25,000
(2) Less: Cost of sales	16,100	15,500	14,125
Gross Profit	$16,400	$11,625	$10,875
(3) Selling, general and administrative expenses	3,850	3,750	2,900
(4) Research and development	1,200	1,000	800
(5) Depreciation	550	500	400
(6) Amortization	10	10	10
(7) Total Operating Expenses	$ 5,610	$ 5,260	$ 4,110
(8) Operating income	10,740	6,365	6,765
(9) Interest expenses	250	200	175
(10) Pretax income	$10,540	$ 6,165	$ 6,590
(11) Income tax	2,500	1,175	2,000
(12) **Net Income**	**$ 8,040**	**$ 4,990**	**$ 4,590**
(13) Earnings per share of common stock (5,000,000 shares)	$ 1.61	$ 1.00	$ 0.92

After revenues, the statement examines the cost of sales: these expenses include raw materials, supplies, labor, overhead and other indirect manufacturing costs. Other expenses are listed under "selling, general and administrative"—expenses attributable to salaries, advertising, public relations, and so forth. Other items to be included are research and development costs, depreciation, and amortization.

These operating expenses are then deducted from the gross profit (revenues minus the cost of sales) to arrive at operating income. From that figure, interest expenses and taxes are subtracted to find the company's net income.

When that figure is divided by the number of common stock outstanding, you arrive at the earnings per share. If there was a loss, there would be no earnings per share, but a loss per share. Depending on corporate policy, some of those earnings may be distributed as dividends, but only after any dividends are first distributed to all the preferred shareholders.

As with the balance sheet, there is room for discretionary interpretation of the information that is provided. For example, what kind of depreciation is used? Depreciation is a non-cash expense, but clearly a necessary cost if the business is to replace aging assets. Straight-line depreciation is a common and conservative way of charging expenses over the life of the equipment. But it is also possible to use forms of accelerated depreciation that subtract larger sums from income, subsequently lowering the tax liability and of course showing lower earnings. A similar issue exists with research and development costs: Are they capitalized over time or are they written off in the year they are incurred?

Though both the balance sheet and income statement are attested to by independent accountants, there is still room for interpretation. The auditor's statement appears to be a pro forma declaration, but an investor should be cautious here as well. A nationally recognized certification may hold greater authority than one from an unheard-of local CPA. However, auditors, even though paid by the business, may append a conditional statement to the standard two paragraphs, that attest to the preparation to conform with "generally accepted accounting principles applied on a consistent basis." A third or fourth paragraph should alert the investor that all is not well, either because of legal problems, insufficient capital or some unspecified problem.

Such a certification is called a qualified one. Thus, if you read that generally accepted accounting principles "contemplate the realization of assets and liquidation of liabilities in the normal course of business" but in this specific company "recovery of the capital assets is dependent upon future events, the outcome of which is currently undeterminable," a light bulb should start to flash warning signals in your mind. If you read other euphemisms for trouble, such as "successful completion of the company's development program . . . is dependent upon obtaining adequate financing," and "if the ultimate resolution of the uncertainties described in the preceding paragraph . . . , " watch out—you are dealing with a highly dubious situation.

Change in Financial Position

The last major item in most annual reports describes the change in financial position, a statement of cash flows, that is the sources and application of funds. This statement provides a transition from the income statement to the balance sheet, indicating where the monies went and how the company financed its business. A cash flow statement usually covers three fiscal years for comparison's sake. Three categories are summarized:

1. *Source of funds from operating activities:* net income, depreciation, amortization and other adjustments from non-cash items.
2. *Application of funds for operations:* capital expenditures, proceeds from sale of assets, partnership acquisition and other joint ventures, purchase of research and development and assumption of other liabilities.
3. *Funds used (or provided) by investment or financing activities:* issuance of long-term debt, proceeds from sale of common stock, proceeds from options and warrants and return of capital as a result of reorganization.

The results are increases or decreases in working capital and a new configuration of assets and liabilities. Annual reports may also provide other tables—on taxes, inventories, investments in joint ventures, leases, pension plans and business segments—as well as illustrated graphs and photographs. A real gold mine for the potential investor is often overlooked—notes to the consolidated financial statement. They can reveal many things a corporation would prefer not to disclose but is obliged to do so, if only in small print: the cost of future leases, pending litigation and related party transactions. Many sophisticated investors denigrate the glossy annual report as too self-serving, which it indeed is. However, there are nuggets occasionally strewn among the platitudes.

Y·O·U·R   M·O·V·E

- Before buying any common stocks, look at the balance sheet and the income statement to evaluate the stability and creditworthiness of the business, as well as the revenues.
- Compare the results of a number of years to obtain a sense of continuity. Companies that show constant and steady increases are more valuable than one with erratic earnings.
- Calculate the debt-to-equity relationship to see if the business is too highly leveraged. Avoid companies that have more than one-third debt, except perhaps in that portion of your portfolio targeted for more speculative issues.
- Check the auditor's statement to see that nothing untoward is present and that the statement conforms to generally accepted accounting principles. Any explanatory comments are cause for further examination.

• 4 •

The Critical Ratios Revealed

The annual report, plus data from secondary sources, gives most of the information necessary for fundamental security analysis. Clearly, there are many valuable numbers for comparisons and for the construction of tables, graphs, and ratios. Since not all numbers are equal, an investor must concentrate on the important ones. While importance, like beauty, is often in the eye of the beholder, the financial world does have priorities, attributing more value to some than to others.

Perhaps the most valuable goal of fundamental analysis is to determine the true worth of a company and then establish whether its value is reflected in the stock market. That is not the whole story—if it were, it would be a static exercise. Since markets and security analyses are anticipatory mechanisms, it is necessary to appreciate the dynamics of the financial world. One is forever shooting at a moving target composed of not only the fundamentals, but other factors as well. Before looking at the nonnumerical conditions, let's examine some basic arithmetic as summarized in five categories: liquidity and credit; effective management and asset allocation; profitability; leverage and solvency; and market value and miscellany.

ᴅITY AND CREDIT

ₐneet primarily reports on the liquidity of
ₗan it meet its obligations in the normal course
ₑss? What will happen if times are tight? Two key
ₗₒs answer these questions. The *current ratio* is the broad
measure of a company's liquidity. It is obtained by dividing
the current assets by the current liabilities. In the case of
High-Tech Tools for the last fiscal year:

$$\frac{17,500,000}{8,045,000} = 2.18$$

Compared to the previous year of:

$$\frac{13,850,000}{6,450,000} = 2.15$$

Some slight improvement. The dollar difference between current assets and current liabilities is referred to as
the company's net working capital.

The other key ratio is a more stringent test of liquidity,
termed the *acid-test ratio* (or the *quick ratio*). It takes only
the current assets that can be turned into usable funds—
cash, marketable securities and short-term investments,
and accounts receivable—divided by current liabilities. In
our case, the quick ratio for the most recent fiscal year is:

$$\frac{9,500,000}{8,045,000} = 1.18$$

And the previous year was:

$$\frac{7,500,000}{6,450,000} = 1.16$$

The current ratio and the quick ratio both tend to fall within general industry norms. While it is different from industry to industry, a current ratio of 2 is considered healthy. The same is true of the quick ratio, where 1 is viewed favorably. While these two ratios represent liquidity, they really speak to the businesses' credit. Respectable current and quick ratios are primary considerations in bank lending. Poor ratios (such as a current ratio of 1 or less, and a quick ratio of less than .75) indicate a cash squeeze or working capital shortage. Excessively rich ratios indicate that management is less efficient than it should be in employing the company's resources.

Moreover, it is a red flag to roving raiders that the company is sitting on assets that might be ripe for plucking through a leveraged buyout and subsequent dissolution of the firm. Individual investors of modest means are in no position to launch a takeover, but much of the merger and acquisition activity in the Eighties has concentrated on such asset ploys. Individuals attracted to this form of investing (for some it is usually little more than following the reported activities of some prominent individuals or groups), might pay attention to these two key ratios.

EFFECTIVE MANAGEMENT AND ASSET ALLOCATION

The balance sheet, in conjunction with the income statement, also tells how effectively the business is turning over its product. This *inventory turnover ratio* is calculated by dividing the cost of sales (from the income statement) by the average inventory—a figure obtained by taking the previous year's inventory and the current year's and dividing by two. Thus for High Tech Tools:

$$\frac{16,100,000}{(7,500,000 + 6,000,000 \div 2 = 6,750,000)} = 2.39$$

Some companies turn over their inventory faster than industry standards, indicating a more aggressive management. A series of turnover figures will show whether the trend is improving or deteriorating.

Another indicator of effective management is to measure how efficiently the business's fixed assets are being used—the *fixed asset turnover ratio*. This figure is arrived at by dividing net sales by the average of total fixed assets. For an average, use figures from two consecutive years and divide by two.

$$\frac{32,500,000}{(8,000,000 + 6,500,000 \div 2 = 7,250,000)} = 4.48$$

Finally, another ratio of efficiency is the *average receivables turnover*, or how much time long it takes the company to collect its due bills. This is determined by dividing net sales by average receivables to calculate the turnover, then dividing 365 days by that figure to arrive at the average collection period. This ratio is probably not as meaningful as it once was, since recent bouts of inflation have made everyone conscious of the time value of money. It is now a general unspoken rule of most business organizations to delay their payables and dun for their receivables immediately.

Income statements report on the company's profitability over the years. They answer the question of how dynamic the business is—is it a situation that is likely to show real growth or is it a plodding and timorous company? Balance sheet analysis is necessary to tell you if the company is healthy, but only income statements can give you an inkling of how the company will perform in the marathon.

PROFITABILITY

A series of ratios reflects whether the company is a long-distance runner or good only for a 100-yard dash. The single most popular measurement to indicate profitability is *earnings per share*. This figure is, quite simply, the bottom line: the net income available for common stock, divided by the number of shares of common stock outstanding. (Companies are also obliged to report the figure for subsequent full dilution when rights, warrants, options and other equivalents are exercised.) For High-Tech Tools the earnings per share for the last year was:

$$\frac{\$8,040,000}{5,000,000\,\text{shares}} = \$1.61$$

That was a 61 percent increase over the previous year, a far better showing than the year before when earnings were up only 9 percent.

The question facing the analyst and investor is, why the sudden surge? What event, condition or even change in accounting procedures was responsible for the improvement? To understand whether it was a one-time fluke (a fire at a competitor's factory), a special condition (sale of assets) or the result of a careful long-term business plan, you have to look at the top lines. The relation of revenues to earnings is best seen through a few ratios. To determine how well the company is doing, especially compared with others in the same industry, you should calculate the gross profit margin, that is, gross profits divided by net sales (revenues after returns and adjustments):

$$\frac{\$16,400,000}{\$32,500,000} = 50.5\%$$

Compared to the previous year it was a marked improvement:

$$\frac{\$11,625,000}{\$27,125,000} = 42.8\%$$

Some analysts prefer to use the *net profit margin* (net income divided by net sales) since it indicates the percentage profit for each dollar of revenues:

$$\frac{\$8,040,000}{\$32,500,000} = 24.7\%$$

In the previous year:

$$\frac{\$4,990,000}{\$27,125,000} = 18.4\%$$

While the above ratios tell the investor how profitable the company is, both compared with others in the same industry as well as internally, it is necessary to put profitability in perspective. How much capital was required to get those results? In brief, did the company succeed on modest assets or did it require a massive amount of money? What was the return on assets? This ratio, popularly called *return on investments*, is calculated by dividing operating income by total assets:

$$\frac{\$10,740,000}{\$27,300,000} = 39.3\%$$

This was an extraordinary return, far better than that of the previous year, though that was certainly respectable.

$$\frac{\$6,365,000}{\$21,750,000} = 29.3\%$$

Some analysts prefer to know the *return on equity* (ROE), since it is more critical in evaluating the value of stock investment. The return on equity is figured by dividing net income by the stockholders' equity (both common and preferred):

$$\frac{\$8,040,000}{\$44,195,000} = 18.2\%$$

Again, it was an improvement over the past year:

$$\frac{\$4,990,000}{\$40,850,000} = 12.2\%$$

Returns on assets and equity reveal how well management performed. It can also answer the question as to whether the company should borrow more money to expand. If it can make more money on borrowed funds than the interest rate on the funds, it might be worthwhile. However, leveraging the company's equity tends to increase the variability of the common stock's earnings. This "trading on the equity" is a two-edged sword, wonderful under strong business conditions and up markets, but devastating when the economy weakens as the new debt burden erases modest earnings.

LEVERAGE AND SOLVENCY

These ratios of profitability lead to the next consideration for the investor: How leveraged is the company (or, in other words, does the company have a high percentage of debt to equity?) Does the capitalization ensure solvency? Management can, of course, increase or decrease both borrowed funds and common stock. Either action will have a direct impact on the market: For example, an announced buy-back program of equity tends to put a floor under the stock, while issuing more stock is often believed to be a depressant on the market. An investor should be aware of a company's current level of capitalization, since it indicates potential price action. Stocks of debt-free companies tend to exhibit less volatility than those of highly leveraged companies. Volatility, however, is not due solely to capitalization: It is possible to find companies with high beta (that is, the relationship of the movement of a stock's price swings to the Standard & Poor's 500) without any debt, but they are the exception rather than the rule.

For High-Tech Tools, the capitalization is:

Percentage		Amount
20.7	Bonds	$ 7,500,000
2.7	Preferred Stock	1,000,000
13.8	Common Stock	5,000,000
0.4	Additional Paid-in Capital	150,000
62.2	Retained Earnings	22,500,000
98.8	Total Capital	$36,150,000

With 21 percent of the company's capital from bonds, or bonds representing 27 percent of the debt-to-equity capitalization, High-Tech Tools is not highly leveraged. Should the capital base change so that capitalization consists of 50 percent bonds and 50 percent stock, the additional borrowed funds might jeopardize the company's earnings. In recent years, debt has become more fashionable (but perhaps will be no less dangerous in the next recession) and many companies now have a third of their capital in debt instruments. Debt service charges are tax deductible to a company, while dividends are not. A brief glimpse of the effect of leverage on earnings illustrates the danger.

A company with $1 million on net income, 1 million shares outstanding, and $500,000 of after-tax debt service on its bonds will earn:

$$\frac{\$1 \text{ million income} - \$500,000 \text{ debt service}}{1 \text{ million shares}} = \$0.50$$

If the company's income increases to $2 million, there is a disproportionate increase:

$$\frac{\$2 \text{ million} - \$500,000}{1 \text{ million shares}} = \frac{1.5}{1} = \$1.50$$

Net income went up 100 percent, but per share earnings increased by three times. If the company earned $3 million with the same debt service, the earnings would have reached $2.50, or a five-fold increase. And, of course, it works in reverse. If the company earned only $500,000, it would all go to debt service and nothing would be left for the common stockholder. A 50 percent drop in earnings (from $1 million), and equity owners lose 100 percent of their earnings.

Regardless of how much leverage a company employs, the investor must look at one final ratio—the ability of the business to cover its debt service costs. *Debt coverage* is calculated by dividing the operating profit by interest costs. For High Tech Tools:

$$\frac{\$10,790,000}{\$250,000} = 43 \text{ times}$$

That figure is exceedingly comfortable, indicating that even a substantial fall in income would not effect debt service. The company has outstanding $7.5 million in bonds, but is paying only $250,000 in interest costs: At one time it was able to borrow money at 3.33 percent.

MARKET VALUE AND MISCELLANY

Finally, there are few ratios that relate the stated value of the company to the market price of the common stock as seen in the balance sheet and the income statement. If the other measurements are pleasing—they fall within the general parameters of both the historic ratios for the company and are not out of line with the specific industry—then one must come back to the central question: Is the company underpriced, overpriced or fairly priced in the marketplace? A few ratios help with the evaluation.

Price Earnings Ratio

The *price earnings ratio* (P/E) is one of the most culled figures of investors and analysts. It is simply the market price per share divided by the earnings per share. The figure given in the daily newspaper is one based on *trailing earnings*, that is, the earnings for the last 12 months. Earnings for the current fiscal year may require estimates of a couple of quarters. Clearly, the P/E for the next year is a projection, a guesstimate based on any number of factors—interviews of management, current-year trends, business conditions as viewed by the government or competitors, prices of commodities, labor markets, etc. Estimated P/Es are subject to wide fluctuations. Perhaps the best an investor can expect is to consult the consensus estimate as published by the statistical services and brokerage houses.

A low P/E is an indication of a company with problems or slow growth potential. Stocks in some industry groups carry relatively modest P/Es, so it is far more important to examine intra-industry P/Es and better still to look at the P/Es of the company itself over the past three to five years. Whether the company's shares are a better buy when the P/E is low or when the P/E is high is debatable. The answer must be conditioned on prospects and promises.

If the outlook is considerably rosier than the P/E would suggest, the stock may be a good buy. On the other hand, a high P/E suggests that company affairs are indeed quite rosy at the present. Are they likely to get much better, to push a P/E of 20 to say 25? Some cynics suggest that an unusually high P/E by historic standards is a wonderful alarm call to either sell the stock or to sell it short.

The level of P/E ratios has much to do with the age of the business cycle. The stocks of some companies trade at their lowest P/Es during a recession when no one wants them and prospects are gloomy, and at their highest when the economy is strong, the cycle is at its mature stage and everybody wants to own stock. They look bad to investors in the former period and best in the latter, but this simple strategy is more likely to disappoint than succeed.

However, it is more complicated than the above scenario suggests. Toward the end of a business cycle—the recession—some of the cyclical stocks (housing, autos, steel, consumer durables and capital goods) begin to show high P/E ratios. Presumably they are too highly priced, judging from the P/E. In reality, earnings have been squeezed by poor business conditions, but managements have trimmed the excesses of the previous cycle and are ready to partake in the next one. It is time to buy those companies despite their seemingly high P/Es.

Book Value

In another chapter we discuss book value as an indicator of intrinsic worth—total stockholders' equity (less preferred) divided by shares outstanding. In the current market, the resulting figure averages about a half of the market price. Some stocks, however, trade at or below their book value, especially financial organizations. When companies, other than financial ones, trade at those levels, there is usually a special reason. If that condition appears to be a temporary one, then buying the stock might be considered. If the company falls on further hard times and seeks liquidation, you may well be in a fail-safe position since you should recoup your investment.

Dividend Ratios

Finally, the dividend ratios will not tell you whether the shares are underpriced or overpriced, but will give you an idea of likely trading parameters. The *dividend yield* is the dividend per share divided by the market price. A company with a dividend of $1 selling at $21 has a dividend yield of 4.76 percent. The company's shares do not sell only on the yield. Companies with a long history of payouts are reluctant to dramatically alter them, but sometimes circumstances are beyond their control. Thus the dividend acts as something of a floor for the market price—conditioned by the prevailing interest rates.

Another dividend ratio measures the *payout:* the dividends per share divided by the earnings per share. Investment grade and/or blue chip companies may have payouts that exceed 50 percent—a dollar for the company and a dollar for the shareholder. Some growth companies pay out nothing, insisting that shareholders nevertheless are getting their due from the increased potential and value of the company. Many aggressive investors prefer companies that have no payout, since there is no tax liability. Income investors are likely to avoid those companies.

Both dividend ratios—yield and payout—are revealing in themselves, but take on more significance when a trend of consecutive increases from year to year is apparent. Portfolios with dividend yields higher than that of the Dow Jones Industrial Average are likely to be less volatile in daily market action than ones with low yields. However, such portfolios are more yield-sensitive and will react to changes in inflation and interest rates.

Cash Flow and Price to Sales

Fundamental analysis has not changed a great deal over the years, but there are fashions and fads. Wall Street has a history of focusing almost exclusively on one set of figures as if they were a Rosetta Stone. For a while, money supply figures released by the Fed were given the highest priority, to be replaced by interest rates, then trade balance figures, federal deficits and unemployment statistics. Each fad is eclipsed by new concerns. Of late, two ratios that have attracted a great deal of attention are *cash flow* and *price to sales*. Cash flow is net income plus the noncash items that are part of operating expenses such as depreciation and amortization. Cash flow is a company's total source of funds. Cash flow is an indication of a company's ability to fund its own growth internally—the preferred way rather than take on more debt or dilute earnings by issuing more stock. Cash flow also determines a corporation's dividend policy: Earnings may be temporarily weak, but as long as cash flow holds up, there is not likely to be a change in dividends. *Cash flow per share* is a handy figure to compare companies with, since it is a broader and truer measurement of company earnings.

Some analyses claim that the price to sales ratio (PSR) is a better indicator than the more common P/E ratio. Figuring the company's sales per share is calculated by dividing the sales total in the last 12 months by the number of shares outstanding, then dividing that quotient into the stock's price. This is a useful measure for companies that may be in their early development, when sales are booming but earnings have yet to appear. A high PSR is also an indicator that the company is overpriced—indeed, some analysts think it a better gauge of what not to buy than what to purchase. If a company has a low PSR plus sound fundamentals, it might be an attractive candidate.

The number of ratios just discussed, some dozen-and-a-half, are generally considered the most significant ones for fundamental analysis. There are others, not to mention combinations and permutations of the above. Formulas and ratios, however, can give only a quantitative sense of a business. It is equally important to have a sense of a company's management, the quality of its product or service and the prospects for its future—a number of intangibles that also directly bear on the success of an investment. Getting a "feel" for the company is just as important as understanding the financials. Moreover, an appreciation of how a security performs in the marketplace is the subject of the next section. Timing is as important in investing as it is in comedy—if you get it wrong, no one will be laughing.

Y·O·U·R M·O·V·E

- Set up your own filters to select the right securities and weed out the wrong ones. Choose one critical ratio from each major category reviewed above. For example, the following key ratios are highly regarded in the financial community.

1. Liquidity and credit: The current ratio should be at least 2 to ensure that the business has sufficient money to operate.
2. Management: The inventory turnover ratio will inform you if the business is thriving, especially compared to others in the same industry.
3. Profitability: The earnings per share gives an immediate bottom-line appraisal of the company's profit status.
4. Leverage: The debt-to-equity ratio shows whether the company is using too much borrowed money.
5. Market value: The price-earning ratio is a quick evaluation of the company's market value. It is especially useful to compare with other companies in the same field.

- Don't be limited to your key ratios: consider book value, dividend yield, dividend payout, cash flow and price to sales.
- More important than any ratio or number is the quality of management. Research the executive officers to see if you like their management style and whether their goals are your goals. Do they consider themselves as fiduciaries, owners, partners, hired hands or quick-buck artists looking to buyout the corporation to enrich themselves?

• 5 •

Technical Analysis

SUPPLY AND DEMAND

Technical analysis is concerned with a basic law of economics, the law of supply and demand. The graphic representation of stock prices and volume, plus a host of other indicators, will reveal set and established patterns. Since these paradigms repeat themselves, they are particularly useful in determining entrance and exit points for traders and investors.

Sounds simple, but the understanding and execution of technical analysis is not easier than that of fundamental analysis. In its own fashion, it raises new questions while supplying answers that are open to conflicting interpretations. Though some observers find technical analysis ambiguous, it can focus attention on the critical question of timing.

There are many different forms of technical analysis—we shall touch on only the most popular basic ones. Modern technical analysis started with the writings of Charles Dow, an editor and founder of *The Wall Street Journal* at the turn of the century. His articles on stock price movements were codified by William Hamilton (an associate of Dow's and later editor of the *Journal*) in his book *The Stock Market Barometer* and by Robert Rhea (a market participant and author of *The Dow Theory*, published in 1932). Rhea

63

modestly noted "I have no qualification to justify my writing a book on the Dow theory, except the firm conviction that it is the only reasonably sure method of forecasting stock market movements."

As originally conceived, the theory was a reflection of business activity and an attempt to forecast it. Only later did it become a tool for forecasting changes in stock prices. The theory holds that the securities markets are composed of three trends at any given time: the *tide* is the major trend, whether we are in a bull or bear market; the *waves* are of secondary importance, corroborating or negating the major trend; the *ripples* are patternless day-to-day fluctuations. Bull markets in which prices tend to advance last longer than bear markets, in which overall prices fall. The average bull market in the postwar period has lasted 36 months, while the average for bear markets is 15 months. Secondary trends running counter to the primary one last between three weeks and three months.

How does the Dow theory signal a change in that primary trend? It uses two averages, the Dow Jones Industrials and the Dow Jones Transportation (originally the Railroads)—they must confirm each other, that is, by reaching new highs or new lows to maintain the trend. When they no longer confirm, when a divergence between the two indices occurs, a reversal is in the offing. Since the Industrials is an index of the nation's productive capacity, and the Transportation is indicative of the volume of goods being shipped, it stands to reason that the cycle is intact as long as both move in tandem. Divergence occurs when the indices refuse to validate each other's direction.

Technicians chart the indices by examining the peaks and troughs of the waves. If the crest is higher than those preceding it and the trough is also higher than the preceding trough, then the bullish trend is intact. Conversely, when the crest and trough are lower than the preceding ones, the bear market continues. If there is a divergence with the crest higher or lower, but the trough not confirming, it is a guarded signal to be aware of a possible change in the trend. Observers are frequently faced with nonconfirming signals.

A resolution comes when a breakout occurs, the sideways moving average pierces the support level on the downside or the resistance level on the upside. Stock and indices spend a long period in a horizontal trading range as they move through a cycle.

The Dow theory is meant to validate a trend or to suggest caution at a turning point. Some have questioned the accuracy of the Dow theory, since it is meant to interpret business conditions as well as stock prices. There have been confirmations that have not presaged major market declines or recessions. No technical tool is perfect, but it should be remembered that the indices are measuring what has already taken place—it is up to the interpreter to provide a meaningful forecast.

Dow theorists examine the averages with near-religious fervor and do have a substantial and loyal following. It is prudent to pay attention to what is, after all, one of the most widely followed technical theories for at times it almost has the force of a self-fulfilling prophecy.

Technical analysis assumes that there is a cyclicality to the behavior of stock prices, if not to the behavior of individual investors. That is the core case, that patterns repeat themselves and one may profit by anticipating that cyclicality. The parallel to the business cycle is inescapable. From bull market to bear market and back, a number of stages may be ascertained from charts of individual stocks or indices. These stages are called accumulation, congestion, breakout, penetration, distribution and readjustment.

In the first stage, roughly equivalent to revival in the business cycle, stocks are at their cyclical lows. Because stocks are viewed as cheap, they are bought by savvy and knowledgeable investors. Most of the investing public is still recovering from the just-passed recession, disillusioned with the market since many did not see signs of the impending sell-off. Smart investors start to accumulate stocks, believing prices to be cheap. During a period of accumulation, prices move in a horizontal trend, moving, as the axiom has it, "from weak hands to strong ones." Each stage is accompanied by a channel or trendline that marks the top of the trading range (the resistance area) and the bottom (the support area). The cycle moves to the next stage when those trendlines are violated.

After the accumulation stage has lasted for a while, prices meander in a congestion area until they break out. An upside penetration indicates that buyers have overwhelmed sellers, who are now demanding (and receiving) higher prices. Buyers reluctantly accumulate and prices start an upward trend, which eventually recovers all the lost ground from the last cycle and eventually starts to make new highs. This record stage, rather like the business expansion stage, is profitable and attracts new investors and speculators. Soon this stage exhausts itself and an equilibrium develops between buyers and sellers at higher price levels. At this stage, however, rather like in a mature business cycle, profit taking sets in—the old buyers are now the new sellers—distributing their earlier purchases.

The stage, distribution, is eventually replaced by a disequilibrium as sellers panic to get out and prices penetrate support levels. This final stage is a readjustment of prices downward—in business cycle terms a contraction and subsequent recession. Technicians, of course, are not interested in business conditions—the reasons why stock produce these configurations according to fundamentalists—only in these formations, graphically demonstrated.

FIGURE 5.1   Accumulation and Breakout Pattern

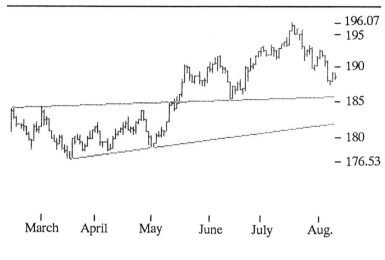

CHARTING THE PATTERNS

While the cycle is remarkably similar from company to company, the graphic formations are not quite parallel. Technicians use a number of recognizable formations to indicate where they are in the cycle and what is to be expected. Bar charts are most commonly used, since their construction is simple and the message is obvious. The prices are marked on the vertical line and contain three pieces of information: high and low prices for the day (or week) and the closing, represented by the cross bar. When continually plotted, a distinctive pattern emerges. The accumulation and congestion pattern forms a channel, with prices contained by a top resistance line and a bottom support line (Figure 5.1).

When a breakout occurs, penetration of the top and bottom must be made in sufficient volume to convince the chartist that it is not a false breakout. Some chartists also keep volume indicators, which tend to confirm price activ-

FIGURE 5.2 Breakout on Volume

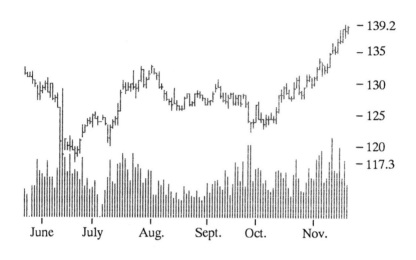

ity. A breakout on thin or even normal volume is suspect, while heavy volume would confirm the breakout (Figure 5.2).

An upside breakout will develop a new trend and form a channel. Once the channel is identified, buying at the bottom of a channel and selling at the top is worthwhile. But the channel's breakout also anticipates the extent of the advance by extending a trendline from the previous high through the breakout high. Similarly, the bottom channel line can be projected by extending a line from the last low to the latest low. Prices will likely remain within the new channel. A basic assumption held by technicians is that the market follows trends. One analyst has said that "the trend is your friend." Another assumption dear to technicians (as it was to Newton) is that a trend in motion tends to remain that way unless changed by some new force.

If the trend changes, for whatever reason, a new pattern will develop. If the stock has made new highs and distribu-

FIGURE 5.3   Head and Shoulders Pattern

– 232.04
– 220
– 210
– 200
– 190
– 180
– 170
– 158.25

M A M J J A S O N D J F M A M J J A S O N D J F M A M J J

tion is the next likely stage, the trend will start to trace one of a number of reversal patterns. The most common is the classic *head and shoulders*: the head is the stock's acme, while the shoulder of consequence is the right shoulder, which breaks below the trendline (Figure 5.3).

Another reversal pattern is the *triple top*, where the stock surges three times to a resistance line and is turned back each time. The belief is that if it cannot go up, the stock must come down (Figure 5.4).

A third reversal is less dramatic as prices roll over gradually, forming an *inverted saucer* (Figure 5.5).

Clearly, these reversal patterns work equally well turned on their heads—indicating a reversal at bottoms.

Technicians look for other patterns as well: reversals remain within an up trend or down trend; gaps where prices jump, either trading at above the previous day's high or below the previous day's low; descending or ascending triangles; coils; pennants; flags; and so on. Each formation has a meaning to the interpreter, but as in so many other

FIGURE 5.4   Triple Top Pattern

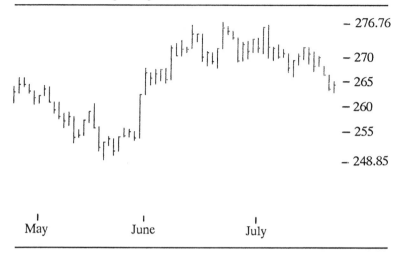

cases in the market, there are often strong contrary opinions as to what the formations mean.

MAJOR INDICATORS

Technicians use other indicators to confirm their interpretations. First and foremost is volume. Many observers believe that price follows volume, that the first signs of awakened interest in a comatose security will be a jump in volume before a jump in price. Volume is a true indicator of supply and demand. The market is considered strong when volume increases as prices rise, and weak when volume expands as prices fall. Conversely, the market is considered weak when volume declines as prices rise, and strong when volume declines as prices fall.

Volume is particularly important as stocks make new highs or lows. If volume is lower than in the previous high, this constitutes a bearish sign, and a reversal may be in the

FIGURE 5.5   Inverted Saucer Pattern

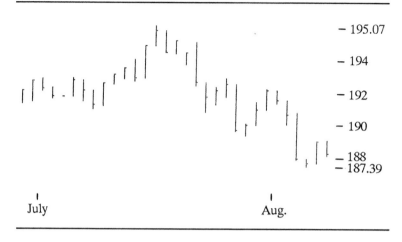

offing. And if volume is lower than in the preceding trough, this should be considered a bullish sign, since prices seemingly do not wish to work lower. A reversal is imminent on the upside when volume dries up and prices fail to make new highs—this means that stock is exhausted and that investors should look for the exits, since the bull market may be over.

A bear market may be over when a *selling climax* occurs after stocks have been pounded on heavy volume. In a selling climax, volume dramatically increases and prices fall to new lows, but the volume indicates sellers are exhausted; a reversal is imminent. On the upside, a selling climax is known as a *blowoff* (Figure 5.6).

Besides the raw volume figures, technicians manipulate the figures to give them extra meaning. *On-balance volume* attempts to measure the excess of up volume against down volume over a day or a month. The purpose is to see if demand volume is greater than supply volume, even if the price remains unchanged. This up tick and down tick strength is calculated by various financial services and is

FIGURE 5.6   Blowoff Pattern

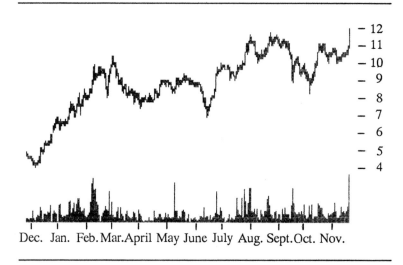

Dec.   Jan.   Feb. Mar. April May June July Aug. Sept. Oct. Nov.

accessible by personal computer. Other volume figures include the *percentage of shares outstanding* traded on a weekly basis and the *liquidity* volume ratio, which measures how much dollar volume is required to move a stock's price up or down one percentage point. Different statistical services have their own proprietary volume indicators to help confirm price movements or illustrate divergences.

Other technical indicators are followed as well. *Moving averages* try to determine whether present price action is in line with or in opposition to previous price behavior. It is arrived at by averaging a series of days (either 200 days or 30 days are most common), then adding the new number to those already averaged after omitting the first number of the series to obtain the new average. Should the moving average rise after a decline and the daily price move above the moving average line, the time is right to buy.

On the other hand, if the daily price tends toward or slices definitively through the moving average line, or both, selling should be in order. A moving average line is

FIGURE 5.7 Moving Average

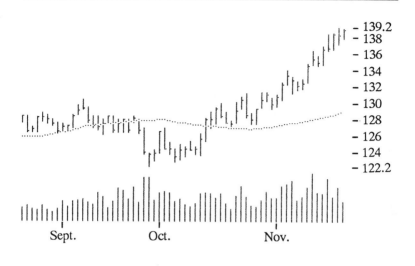

created in an attempt to identify the current trend by comparing it with the moving average trend to see if the trend is still intact. Moving averages that are tightly constructed, within 10 to 30 days, mirror the daily activity quite closely, while longer-term moving averages are perhaps better at indicating major reversals (Figure 5.7).

Oscillators are still another tool in the kit bag that indicates momentum: an oscillator moves from a central value to a maximum or minimum value. When prices advance, the oscillator rises and conversely falls when prices retreat. Oscillators are calculated by comparing the performance of two items by subtracting one from the other at each and every point on the chart. The usual components are two moving averages of different time periods. When the oscillator crosses the mid-value or zero line, it is a sign to buy or sell, depending on its direction. An oscillator is also an early warning signal: Should there be a significant

FIGURE 5.8   Oscillator

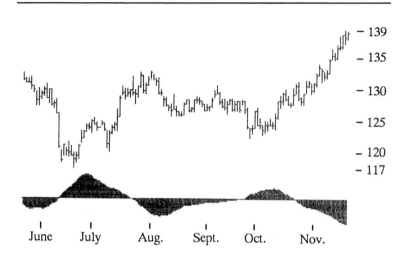

divergence between the price and an extreme oscillator, a correction is due (Figure 5.8).

Another common indicator is the *advance-decline line,* arrived at by calculating the net difference between the number of stocks rising and the number falling. A measure of the breadth of the market, it can be plotted against a general average to see if the advance-decline line is confirming the price trend or is diverging from it.

Another similar measurement is the number of new highs and the number of new lows. A trend remains in place as long as one side dominates the other by a 2-to-1 ratio. A listless or dull market will find them about even.

Finally, two measurements are believed to reflect superior information by the participants. The short interest ratio is the number of short sales by the public, divided by the average monthly sales. A high ratio is considered bullish and a low one bearish. This ratio, however, is perhaps less indicative than it once was, since people who have the disposition to sell short now use alternative instruments to accomplish their ends, such as options and futures.

Short sales by stock exchange specialists are still considered excellent prognosticators. The specialists are charged by the exchanges to both make an orderly market and to step in to act as a broker's broker. In the first instance, the specialist keeps a book of limit orders from investors; with this knowledge, the specialist must buy or sell to stabilize prices and counter trends. To accomplish this, specialists short stocks. The ratio of specialists' short sales to the total number of short sales on the exchange is thought to be highly indicative. A high percentage of members' short sales is considered bearish, while a low percentage is considered bullish.

Corporate insiders are another privileged group of market participants, and they are obliged to report their stock transactions to the SEC. In addition, major investors who buy more than 5 percent of a company's equity (or any class of securities) are also obliged to file an information form, a 3D, with the SEC within 10 days of their purchase. Many investors monitor these filings (and often imitate them), since they believe that insiders are most knowledgeable.

Insiders no doubt buy on pleasing prospects, but there is little evidence to suggest that company insiders have better-than-average portfolio performance. Perhaps they are really too close to the business. Insider selling is the result of not only potential hard times but the need for cash to pay for real estate, college tuition, medical emergencies and other expenses. Insiders buy expecting to make money, but it is never clear why they sell.

Technical analysis charts what is happening to stock prices—virtually in real time thanks to personal computers, broadcast and cable television, radio transmissions and other communication devices. This instant access has leveled the playing field for many investors. With fundamental analysis, you are never the first to know of basic developments that cause price movements. With technical analysis, all interested parties see the workings of supply and demand at the same time.

While we have touched upon some of the techniques technicians use to measure trends and forecast price movements, there is not necessarily agreement on what is observed and what it means. Personal interpretation is as meaningful in one form of analysis as another. By employing both, the chances of success are immeasurably increased.

Y·O·U·R   M·O·V·E

- Though you may not become a practicing technician, you should appreciate the repetitive patterns in the stock market. By using technical analysis in conjunction with fundamental analysis, you will improve your trading.
- Familiarize yourself with the half-dozen major technical indicators: accumulation, congestion, breakout, penetration, distribution and readjustment.
- If you wish to monitor your position, especially the more speculative and/or volatile issues, keep charts as to their daily or weekly activities.
- Study volume indicators to confirm chart patterns.
- By keeping an advance decline and a moving average chart, you can obtain visual confirmation of market moves on a current basis. These are especially important at turning points in the market.

• 6 •

Strategies for Superior Performance

AVERAGING UP

Paying attention to the business cycle is a classic approach to the key problem of timing purchases and sales. However, there are other equally successful ways to invest that rely on different techniques and philosophies. Some investors use one method, some another, but there is no reason not to mix them. One truism that appears valid in the investment world is the simple observation that no one technique works all the time. Just as you diversify a portfolio with 8, 10 or 15 companies in order to eliminate company risk, it is wise to consider and implement different approaches.

One answer to the problem of timing is to pass: It is too difficult and too tenuous to place much faith in it in the view of some. Ignore timing and implement a strategy that does not rely on the vagaries of the business cycle and a host of sometimes confusing leading indicators. By using a fixed formula, the issue of when to buy and when to sell is not subject to a judgment call.

Dollar cost averaging is perhaps the most popular of these plans. By regularly purchasing the same dollar amount of securities over a long period, it is possible to buy more shares at low prices than at high prices. Thus the investor accumulates more low-priced shares than high-priced shares. This is a systematic method of buying shares at an average cost that is lower than the average price of those shares.

For example, an investor decides to buy $1,000 of stock each quarter of the ABC Company. Its shares are $50 each at the start of his dollar cost averaging. His program might look like the one in Table 6.1.

At the end of two years, the investor spent $8,000 for 125 shares worth (@$90) $11,250. With $8,000 he or she could have bought 160 shares at $50 initially (if the money had been available), which would have been worth $14,400. At the other extreme, an investor could have bought 89 shares for $8,000 at the end of the period. Clearly, low stock prices, are better than high stock prices since more shares will be accumulated. This form of investing also works best when there is predictable growth and a real likelihood of higher prices. It works best with volatile issues and it can be used easily with mutual funds in order to provide diversity.

This system ensures that the investor will not load up with high-priced issues. When prices decline, the damage to the portfolio will not be as great as it otherwise might have been.

There are some disadvantages as well: Commission charges for odd lots (less than a hundred shares) can be high; there is a natural reluctance to buy when prices are high; there is also a natural sense to sell out when prices are depressed rather than maintain the program; and dedication to constant buying of a company's shares may blind one to problems that develop within that firm over time.

TABLE 6.1   Dollar Cost Averaging for the ABC Company

Quarter	Price Per Share	No. of Shares	Shares Cost
1st	$ 50.00	20	$1,000
2nd	43.00	23	1,000
3rd	55.00	18	1,000
4th	66.66	15	1,000
5th	70.00	14	1,000
6th	80.00	12	1,000
7th	85.00	12	1,000
8th	90.00	11	1,000
Total	$539.66	125	$8,000

Average Price   Average Cost Per Share
$539.66 ÷ 8 = $67.46 $8,000 ÷ 125 = $64

OTHER FORMULA PLANS

Other formulas are also useful to the passive investor. The *constant ratio plan* is a simple way to keep equilibrium between common stock and fixed-income investments. You could start a program by dividing your portfolio (or intended portfolio) in half: 50 percent of the value in common stock and 50 percent in bonds. The holdings are evaluated on a regular basis, say, every three or six months. If the stock side increases beyond a given point, say, 60 percent, some stocks are sold. If it declines below 40 percent, some stocks are bought. As prices rise, the profit from the sold stocks is converted into bonds. As stock prices fall, some bonds are sold to buy more shares.

This system keeps the investor balanced and allows for profitable, programmed trading. Obviously a judgment on asset allocation has to be made as to whether 50-50 is appropriate or 90-10 would better serve. This judgment must also be made by employee-shareholders of company pension plans. Many company income-sharing plans require or request the participants to select how their retirement funds are to be balanced for the forthcoming year.

Another variation of a passive investment program is the *constant dollar plan.* An investor establishes a safety point in dollar terms above which he or she will not venture any further funds in common stock. Whether it be $20,000 or $100,000, the safety point is one that keeps his or her portfolio from experiencing too much exposure. The portfolio sells shares if that point is crossed, reinvesting in the more conservative fixed-income side. On the other hand, the portfolio sells bonds and buys shares when the stock side is substantially below the safety point.

DIVIDEND REINVESTMENT PLANS

Dividend reinvestment plans, under which dividends are used to purchase additional shares of stock, are a convenient and inexpensive way to add to holdings. The vast majority of companies do not charge fees for joining the plans; some even offer a discount from the market price. Dividends reinvested through these plans are taxable to the participant (unless they are in tax-deferred accounts), as is the difference between the fair market price and the discounted price. For more information about these plans, contact the company's shareholder relations department for a copy of the plan's prospectus.

Timing in these formula plans is predetermined by the market's actions. It removes the possibility of active intervention on a whim if the plan is rigorously followed. Critics object to the mechanical artificiality of these schemes. They keep investors from fully participating in long and sustained trends in a business cycle. But then, investors wish to be protected from such participation by definition.

They wish to make progress slowly and methodically: the tortoise, after all, did beat the hare.

CAN YOU FIND TRUE VALUE?

Whether you attempt to time your investments or let a fixed formula do the timing for you, most investors are rightly concerned with the fundamentals of the business in which they are investing. They may or may not be concerned with the price action of the shares or the general market—those are the technical considerations. (Technical analysis is covered in Chapter 5.) Primarily, they are interested in value: Are they getting their money's worth with a company's common stock? They are not interested in a number of items that concern and motivate many Wall Street participants, such as business developments, technological breakthroughs, takeover stories, earnings explosions, cash flow, etc. Their sole criterion is to see that the price either reflects the underlying value or is below it. Value investors are not concerned with business cycle or fads; their goal is to buy a dollar's worth of assets for 50 cents. There are a few approaches to this concept, but you must first understand what the indicators of value are.

Security analysis naturally deals with the financial fundamentals of the company in question. These are revealed in both the balance sheet and the income (also known as the profit and loss) statement and are generally summarized in secondary sources. Literally dozens of important facts relate to the value of the company. Some of the more significant ones are:

- Capitalization—the number of shares outstanding, the amount of long-term debt

- Financial position—current assets, current liabilities, cash and equivalent
- Earnings per share—previous years, current year, last 12 months, estimate of the coming fiscal year
- Dividends—the amount in dollars and cents for previous years, the current dividend this year, the dividend in percentage terms

With the basic current and historical information, an investor can then evaluate some of the critical ratios such as current assets to current liabilities, price to earnings, yields, return on equity, etc.

The value investor can employ a number of different techniques to find out what a company is worth, especially when compared with either a broad index, the industry or another company. A warning is in order at this point: Evaluations of assets, such as land, not to mention goodwill, can be misleading, subjective estimates. Moreover, dramatic revaluations, such as after a panic, can further distort true worth.

Book Value

Perhaps the most useful figure is the book value of a corporation. Book value is the company's total assets minus its total liabilities, divided by the number of outstanding shares. If you can purchase shares in a company for less than book value, you are obtaining the hard assets on the cheap, plus the management, organization, distribution, development and research—the very makings of the business free of charge. The difference is the equity or capital that belongs to the stockholders.

$$\text{Book value} = \frac{\text{Total assets} - \text{Total liabilities}}{\text{Number of shares outstanding}}$$

Thus book value and stockholder's equity per share are the same. Companies selling in the marketplace below book value would appear to be bargains, but that is not always so; any list or screen of such companies will reveal a fair number of near-bankrupt, tired, old or desperate companies. You must look beyond simple book value to see that the company is not only viable but turning in a string of reputable earnings.

Book value of the Dow Jones Industrial Average is used by some market observers to indicate whether the market is too high or too low. When the DJIA was selling at or below its book value, such as in 1974, 1978, 1980 and 1982, substantial rallies followed. In January 1983 the DJIA's price-to-book-value was 1.06 as the bull market started. Conversely, when the DJIA sold at more than 50 percent above its book value, it was followed by falling markets. Shortly before the 1987 crash the DJIA was selling at 4.5 times its book value.

Intrinsic Value

Another valuation concept is a variation of the above, first put forth by the father of security analysis, Benjamin Graham, and his coauthor David L. Dodd in their seminal work, *Security Analysis*. Their idea is now called *intrinsic value,* or sometimes *central value.* In a nutshell, a company's current assets must exceed its current liabilities and long-term debt. If the current assets exceed total liabilities (less the market value of any preferred stock outstanding), the difference should be divided by the number of common shares outstanding to obtain the working capital (more precisely called the "net working capital") per share. If the net asset value per share is greater than the price in the market, then the company's shares are undervalued. This is a more stringent valuation model than book value.

Graham also was aware that a company could have intrinsic value but no future. Consequently, as a precaution he insisted that his universe of potential companies have low price-earnings ratios, either a P/E of 7 or one that was roughly 40 percent below that of the P/E of a general index. A low P/E doesn't predict a rosy future—it only serves to protect an investor from an uncertain one.

Present Value

A third valuation model is *present value*, a way of determining the present price by discounting the future. The present value of an asset is directly related to the future cash flow to be thrown off by that asset. There are two variations on this theme. One way of looking at a company's shares is to assume that the current value is the sum of expected future cash return of the shares—the future cash flow is made up of dividends, plus the price of the shares when sold. Working on the assumption that today's dollar is more valuable than next year's, it is only reasonable to discount the distant dollar. How much that discounting factor should be is open to interpretation. One must allow for risk and interest rate fluctuations. Should the discounting rate be 7.5 percent, then the present value of a dollar one year hence is $1 ÷ 1.075 or $0.93. The second variation is to consider the future flow of earnings rather than dividends, but some observers consider retained earnings part of dividends in the sense that what is not paid out is reinvested in the company to be paid out later. The present value, in essence, states that a stock is worth only what you can get out of it. A farmer's ditty has it:

A cow for her milk
A hen for her eggs

And a stock, by heck
for her dividends.

In other words, stock prices are only a reflection of expected dividends—or expected earnings. In either case, the present value concept is flawed. Since there are so many imponderables in attempting to estimate one year out, let alone ten, for common stock the discounted cash return is pure conjecture. The present value approach has far greater value in fixed-rate instruments where there is more certainty as to payment.

Regardless of which value method is used, finding an undervalued company is meaningful only in the context of an industry or the stock market. *Undervalued* and *overvalued* are relative terms; one must check not only past price action, but also present relational criteria.

How do you measure whether a stock is underpriced or overpriced? A couple of generally accepted procedures produce worthwhile results. The most common measurement—and the one ratio conveniently listed in the daily newspaper stock tables—is the price-earnings ratio (P/E). If shares are selling at $25 and have a *trailing* (or latest) 12-month earnings per share (the total earnings divided by the number of shares outstanding) of $2.90, then the price-earnings ratio ($25 ÷ $2.90) is 8.6. To know whether those shares are fairly valued, you need additional information. What is the yearly (or five-year) low and high of the P/E ratio? If it is 5 to 10, clearly the shares are trading toward the high end of the scale. How does the current P/E compare with the DJIA or the S&P 500?

If the general market is selling at 12 times earnings, the shares' P/E is 28 percent below that of the market. Encouraging, but you must know still more. How does it compare with its peers—the other companies within the industry? If the industry is semiconductors, where the nominal P/E is over 20, then the company would be grossly undervalued.

If, however, the industry is banking (where 5 or 6 is considered normal), it might be a bit richly valued. In short, the context is important, since industry groups have their own parameters.

A stock whose market price is below its book value (or intrinsic value or present discounted value), and in addition is selling at a low price-earnings ratio is likely to be an undervalued security. Another way of determining whether a company or the market is a bargain for value-oriented investors is to look at the price-to-dividend ratio. The dividend yield—the dividend per share, divided by the price per share—is a key ratio for conservative investors. After all, among the reasons to buy common stock was the desire for higher yields, higher than the yields of bonds, which were more secure. Risk demanded greater returns.

When dividend yields are high, stocks are likely to be undervalued. Conversely, when dividend yields fall because of a rise in stock prices, some regard this fall as a red flag. The DJIA cannot withstand a 3 percent yield (or less); It has been called the "line of death." A series of years with low yields in the neighborhood of 3 percent invariably end with sharply declining markets.

In other words, low dividend yields (or a lack of dividend growth) are a sign that the stock market is overpriced, as was the case in the late 1920s, 1938, 1965–68, 1971–73 and of course in 1987, when the dividend yield descended to 2.67 percent before the crash (when the market was at 2700). Or to put it slightly differently, historically, Dow stocks have paid out 61 percent of their earnings in dividends. In October 1987, they were paying out only 50 percent—another sign of an overvalued stock market. Norman Fosback in his book *Stock Market Logic* (Dearborn Financial Publishing, Inc., 1991) notes that the dividend yield on the Dow was below 3 percent for just 19 weeks between 1941 and 1975 and "in every case the ensuing one-year market return was sharply negative." In 1987 the

S&P 500 dividend yield fell to 2.5 percent, the lowest it had been in a century. The crash was no surprise to those who follow this indicator.

Value investors cannot be satisfied only with securities selling below their intrinsic or book value. They must also look toward a firm's profitability to ensure that it is indeed a going concern, likely to be more successful in the future than it is in the present. Without that basic assumption, there may be no reason to buy its shares other than to liquidate the company and sell off its assets to realize the book value. That may well be the job of financial syndicates pursuing leveraged buyouts, but it is not the usual role for an individual investor.

THE SEARCH FOR EARNINGS

Value investing has always had a loyal and hard-core following, but for many years it had fallen out of fashion. In strong and prolonged bull markets value investors complain that they cannot find anything "cheap." There are few bargains in booms when virtually everything seems to advance. Such was the case in 1984–87. After the market meltdown, value investing became all the rage again. Value was to be a safeguard against volatility in the minds of many market participants.

One strategy that never goes out of fashion, and indeed should be used with value investing, is the search for corporate profits that are extraordinary. No other fundamental factor is quite so persuasive to professional money managers or has such a great effect on stock prices. After all, the main reason for acquiring shares in a company is the belief that a rise in earnings will cause both an appreciation in the value of the firm as well as an increase in its dividends. Even if the firm does not issue dividends, as is the case with many companies, the retained earnings will increase future earnings and hence share price.

Consequently, Wall Street spends a great deal of time and energy projecting earnings, not only for the next three-month period, but for subsequent years. These earnings expectations or anticipations move stock prices. Indeed, the Institute for Quantitative Research in Finance has published findings that suggest that consensus earnings estimates explained share prices better than historical earnings, book value or sales per share. Stock prices adjust quickly to major new or revised estimates by leading analysts and or major publications. Investors are looking for companies with healthy earnings gains. What moves the market is not so much the level of expectations (those are already in the price) but the change in expectations (which are not in the price). So while earnings estimates tend to lead stock prices, sometimes prices change faster than estimates.

Publication of actual earnings occasionally reveals that consensus estimates are wide of the mark—and the price may move counter to what might be presumed. It is not uncommon to see an earnings report fall short of Wall Street expectations by a few pennies and the price plummet. For example, one of the hottest issues in 1989 was L.A. Gear, a maker of sneakers and sportswear. It fell in price from $42 on the New York Stock Exchange to $33 in a matter of a couple of days when a leading brokerage house reduced its earning's projection from $3.25 to $3.10—a 5 percent fall in an earning's estimate saw the stock lose nearly a quarter of its value. And just as oddly, a company will report earnings of 100 or 200 percent greater than expected with no concomitant price increase.

Earnings estimates are not only subject to wide variations, but fall prey to material facts that no one could predict. When the Alaska pipeline was built, the energy companies allowed for every contingency, or so they thought—all except the fact that the pipeline would block the annual migration of the caribou. The pipeline had to be redesigned, a costly retrofitting that knocked the earnings estimates for a number of energy companies into a cocked hat. And as Anthony Hitschler noted in the *Financial Analysts Journal*, some caribou eventually visit every forecast. Obviously, earnings estimates at the extremes are subject to the greatest correction if the reported earnings are markedly different.

One academic study found that stocks with the biggest positive surprises outperformed the general market by 5.6 percent, and those with the biggest negative surprises underperformed the market by 5.4 percent. Another study suggests that when analysts revise estimates upward to reflect a change in a company's future, there is a 65 percent chance that the trend will also appear in the next two quarters. A similar reaction takes place on the downside, even more strongly. In fact, long before the study an old Wall Street maxim had it that "the first piece of bad news is seldom the last one."

Earnings estimates are made by many brokerage houses (especially the full-service ones), financial publications and statistical services. Since earnings projections are fraught with uncertainty (and the caribou factor), it is prudent to obtain more than one. A number of compilations of estimates from major brokerage houses, investment banks, and magazines are published regularly. Zacks Investment Research publishes in data base form *Corporate Earnings Estimator*, and the Institutional Brokers Estimate System (I/B/E/S) is another data base compiled by the firm of Lynch, Jones & Ryan. The *Wall Street Transcript* publishes the text of analysts' reports, and *Investext* does the same through its electronic library.

Keeping abreast of the latest earnings estimates is critical, but you must also interpret the projections for additional meaning. The first step is to make sure you have the earnings record for the last few years. Earnings growth of 22 percent may sound wonderful for a newly discovered situation, but enthusiasm will vanish if it had a series of recent years where 33 percent growth was the norm. (Some analysts, a decidedly minority view, believe that earnings, like stock prices, follow a random walk: there is no connection between earnings periods, and the study of historical changes is useless as a tool in predicting future changes.)

Historical earnings provide a clue, if nothing else, as to the efficacy of management, how it deals with changing business conditions and market cycles. A trail of earnings is necessary to arrive at important ratios. The premier ratio, as noted before, is price-earnings, the price divided by actual earnings per share (for a trailing fiscal year or the latest 12-month period) or by projected earnings.

While all companies use standard rules as put down by the Financial Accounting Standards Board, it is important to realize that earnings per share may be as reported, adjusted for splits and recapitalization, or stated on a fully diluted basis (all common stock equivalents). High P/Es may indicate that the stock is vulnerable to any reduction of earnings estimates, and low P/Es show that the price has discounted all but an outright business disaster. Conservative investors will try to buy when the P/Es are close to the bottom and sell when they reach the other extreme. Short sellers, of course, would sell high P/Es for the downward ride.

There is great diversity in P/E ratios: they differ from industry to industry; they differ from bull market to bear market; they differ from young companies to mature companies. This diversity is apparent in the recent action of the DJIA:

	Dow
Date	*P/E*
January 3, 1987	16.5
June 1, 1987	19.0
October 2, 1987	19.0
December 4, 1987	13.5
June 1, 1988	15.0
September 1, 1990	11.4
September 5, 1991	19.1

A longer view shows that the variations are quite dramatic:

October 1929	19.1
January 1938	25.1
January 1946	20.0
September 1974	6.1
March 1976	12.2
September 1979	6.4

A prudent investor might consider that the DJIA price has historically averaged at about 14 times earnings. If a P/E of 14 is neutral, 19 might be considered a red flag, a very bearish sign, while a P/E of 10 is very bullish, a sign of clear sailing.

Utilities and financial and insurance companies tend to sell at modest P/Es, while high-technology and growth stocks sell at high ones. At one point, IBM at its acme was selling at 80 times earnings and BankAmerica at 3 times earnings. A new startup in a glamour field, such as Genentech in biotechnology, sold initially at $35, only to touch $89 in its first day's trading as a public company with no earnings in sight for half a dozen years. On the other hand, companies may have high P/E ratios even though earnings have temporarily fallen. In brief, each company is *sui generis*—only by understanding its earnings record as well as its projected earnings estimates can you make a successful decision.

Companies whose earnings are growing at less than 10 percent per year are not likely to show dramatic price performance. Companies exceeding 20 percent per year are turning in superior results that are likely to translate into superior price performance. Finally, consistency of earnings is also a major consideration. The stock of a company whose earnings rise year after year tends to sell at a higher P/E than a cyclical stock.

Y·O·U·R   M·O·V·E

- Defensive investors should consider a number of strategies that are formulated to enter and exit the market in a predetermined manner.
- By buying shares on a periodic basis, it is possible to accumulate more low price shares. This dollar cost averaging requires constant purchasing with a fixed sum for a year or two to be effective.
- Consider balancing your portfolio between stocks and other fixed-income securities. Whatever ratio you decide on, the success of the plan rests on your ability to monitor and act on imbalances.
- Reinvest your dividends to purchase new shares. This is a painless way (if you do not need the dividend income) to increase your stake in the company. Remember that in the long run, a stock's value is a reflection of its dividend stream.
- Earnings and projected future earnings are all important in the stock market. Get the consensus earnings estimate before you buy a company, and then monitor those earnings (and future earnings) to see that there are no surprises.

• *7* •

How To Set Up a Portfolio

ALLOCATING YOUR ASSETS

The latest buzzword among professional money managers is asset allocation—the proper balance of investments in order to optimize portfolio performance. It is an idea no less important to private investors of modest means. For institutional investors it is a question of a tradeoff, maximizing the expected return while minimizing the portfolio's risk. Consequently, they are constantly adjusting the contents of their portfolios to reflect their current judgments of financial markets. They are then obliged to alter their investment mix. The worth of this constant pursuit is debatable—high portfolio turnover does not necessarily lead to outstanding performance, only to higher trading costs.

Individual investors are far better off than professional portfolio managers: They can be more flexible in their attitudes, and more important, they are not under constant scrutiny to see how they measure up against some established benchmark. For individuals, asset allocation should be established at the start of the saving and investment program, and only be modified occasionally.

Let's assume you have $50,000 of liquid assets, funds that are free and clear of any immediate need, except perhaps for some dire emergency. You can choose from a number of scenarios, assuming you are considering some portion of your funds for portfolio investing rather than leaving the funds in a savings bank:

1. The simplest balanced formula is to place half your funds in stocks and half in bonds.
2. A somewhat more defensive strategy would be to keep a third in cash equivalents (money market funds), or Treasury bills, a third in stocks and a third in bonds.
3. If sufficient assets (in excess of $100,000) permit, you could invest a fifth in real estate, a fifth in precious metals and natural resources (stocks), a fifth in international stock, a fifth in U.S. stock, and a fifth in bonds.

Combinations and variations of these strategies can be used to customize your portfolio to fit your personal goals. Nothing is new about diversification, even if it is now called asset allocation. Diversification is an important concept, whether it be among the common stocks in your portfolio or the parts of your overall holdings. Quite simply, diversity equals safety, a fundamental way of hedging your bets. When you diversify, you are reducing your exposure to risk. Moreover, there is some evidence that diversified holdings are likely to perform better than a portfolio of diversified stocks—perhaps not during the most torrid part of a bull market, but overall, through the entire business cycle.

Therefore, asset allocation is an important goal in achieving financial balance and mental equanimity. When bonds are strong, stocks may be weak, or vice versa. Inflation is likely to depress both stocks and bonds, but will act to spur natural resource companies and precious metals. If overseas economies are strong but the domestic one is in a slump, your holdings will receive a fillip from the foreign sector. Should deflation undermine real estate, your deflation oriented securities will provide buoyancy.

One of the most common mistakes investors make is to try to be in the strongest sector at all times, as well as in the strongest equities. There is virtually no way to achieve that end; the normal ebbs and flows of business and finance may not be unfathomable, but they are certainly laced with rapids, crosscurrents and unexpected waterfalls. Striving to constantly be in the strongest sectors invariably leaves you open to the cardinal error of overtrading. This is an expensive and self-defeating indulgence.

One of the prime considerations in managing your funds is not to lose money, but commission fees can eat up your capital at an alarming rate. It is certainly true that the first loss is the easiest (or cheapest) loss. There is a tendency, especially in this new volatile environment, to sell not because of basic changes in situations, but because of the gossamer illusion that the next sector or stock is going to immediately act better. Investing, to reiterate again, is a long-term arrangement, one in which sufficient time is as important as making the current selection.

Whether your equity holdings represent 10 percent or 50 percent or 80 percent of your asset allocation program, it is necessary to have balance and perspective. To customize your portfolio to meet your needs, you must make some fundamental choices as to the kind of investor you are and the type of investments that will fulfill those requirements for your core holdings.

There are three distinct ways of investing:

- For income
- For growth or appreciation
- For safety

INVESTING FOR INCOME

Income investors are not overly concerned about the business cycle, since the companies or agencies in which they are likely to invest are not generally affected by normal business cycles. They are affected, however, by interest rates, which may become inflated in the mature phase of a business boom. Income investors are naturally looking for the highest yield on their funds.

Today, there are a wide variety of choices on the menu, but some care should be taken. The major weakness for income investors is to reach for the very highest yields, whether in stocks or bonds. Yields that are radically higher than prevailing interest rates may be a trap; they reflect the fact that there is a greater element of risk in the instruments. Indeed, they should be a warning to the income investor to abstain from those commitments since they are especially vulnerable to a fall, both in yield and in principal, if the company skips or reduces the dividend, or declares bankruptcy. And it is usually income investors, the ones who most need the monthly or quarterly payments to maintain their living standards, who are most likely to be hurt.

If you are an income investor, you might consider placing half of your funds in high-yield common stock, and the other half in bonds. The purpose of investing for income is to achieve the maximum income consistent with safety of capital. The reason for placing half of your funds in stock is to minimize the effects of inflation, the enemy of the income investor. With an inflation rate of 5 percent, money loses half its purchasing power in a decade. Even when placed in a savings account with average interest rates of 5 1/2 percent, the saver is treading water.

The traditional haven for income investors is common stock of utilities and telephone companies, since they usually not only pay dividends with yields in excess of what banks pay, but may also raise the dividends every year.

Boosting dividends, of course, depends on whether the utility in question is profitable and whether the utility commission in the respective state is likely to allow for rate increases. It is quite possible that within five or ten years the yield on the original funds will have increased considerably, and the equity will have appreciated as well.

Common stock does have a downside: Earnings can remain flat or fall; regulatory authorities may not accede to higher rates; nuclear generation may receive further setbacks. However, the record of utility shareowners over the years has been excellent, even though the shares are sensitive to interest-rate fluctuations. For the income investor, shares of utilities (electric and gas) and telephone companies (Bell companies and others) have served well and are likely to continue to do so. The income investor should consider some of the following utilities:

American Electric Power
Baltimore Gas & Electric
Black Hills
Boston Edison
Cincinnati Gas & Electric
Commonwealth Edison
Consolidated Edison
Delmarva Power & Light
Detroit Edison
Dominion Resources
Duke Power
FPL Group
General Public Utilities
Houston Industries
IPALCO Enterprises
Kansas City Power & Light
Nevada Power
NIPSCO Industries
Niagara Mohawk Power

Northeast Utilities
Northern States Power
Ohio Edison
PSI Holdings
PacifiCorp
Pacific Gas & Electric
Potomac Electric
Public Service Enterprise Group
SCEcorp
San Diego Gas & Electric
Sierra Pacific Resources
Southern Company
Southwest Public Service
TECO Energy
United Illuminating
Wisconsin Energy

American Telephone & Telegraph and the regional bell operating companies also provide stability and reasonable returns:

- Ameritech
- AT&T
- Bell Atlantic
- Bell South
- Nynex
- Pacific Telesis
- Southwestern Bell
- US West

If the income investor wishes to keep a portion of his or her portfolio in bonds, there is a wide range of opportunities:

The income investor can be characterized in two ways:

Secure Income	*Income with Risk*
U.S. Treasury issues	High-yield (junk) bonds
Federal agency issues	Real estate investment trusts
Muncipal bonds	Covertible bonds
AAA corporate bonds	Income bonds
Tax anticipation notes	Collateralized mortgage obligations
Certificates of deposit	
Repurchase agreements	

Most of these issues can be bought individually or through mutual funds or investment trusts that specialize in each genre.

The income investor who needs a regular flow of income to help pay monthly bills should limit income bonds (ones that pay interest only if earned), zero coupon bonds (ones that pay no interest) and certificates of deposit (unless they have a provision for monthly or quarterly payouts). And above all, avoid yields that are out of line with similar investments unless you wish to take on more risk for that additional return.

INVESTING FOR GROWTH

Defining growth is difficult since the concept is a slippery one. What may look like growth in one industry—say, an increase of revenues by 10 percent—may look poky and static in another. This matter must be considered industry by industry and company by company. What can be said with assurance is that earnings of a growth company not only rise faster than its peers but that its business is not generally subject to the normal cyclical downturns of the business cycle.

Growth companies and industries seem to move to the tune of a different drummer, regardless of the economic weather. Furthermore, their valuations, their price-earnings ratios for instance, are linked to projected growth rates. Disappointment, whether real or imagined, inevitably drops the market valuation rather dramatically, just as unexpected optimistic projections raises that valuation. In recent years, growth company evaluations have exceeded the price-earnings ratio of the S&P 500 by 50 to 100 percent.

Core holdings for a growth portfolio should encompass these industries that have spurred the economy, the ones that have been on the cutting edge of change and technological advantage: biotechnology, computers, energy, semiconductors, telecommunications, robotics, media and the service sector, from fast food to financial services.

Growth companies can also be found in industries that are normally thought of as not belonging to the growth sector. For example, within the steel industry (generally thought of as a cyclical industry, beside the fact that it has had intense foreign competition), a number of newer mini-steel mills perform in extraordinary fashion. Within the garbage and refuse collection business, a number of companies have led in environmentally sound solutions for a heretofore backward industry. In the old feed-and-seed agricultural business, genetic engineering has revolutionized a dormant sector. In brief, there are growth companies and investor opportunities within many old-fashioned and sleepy industries.

A portfolio dedicated solely to growth is certainly appropriate during your working career, when building capital is a foremost consideration. However, aggressive pursuit of capital gains can leave you with very volatile investments. Invariably, you take on far greater risks than you might with a balanced portfolio, one dedicated only to income or safety. It is particularly important that a growth investor diversify among industries since even the most successful ones have had a history of falling out of favor for periods of time.

INVESTING FOR SAFETY

This may sound redundant, since a cardinal rule of investing is to safeguard the principal. That, in a phrase, separates investing from speculating. However, in the new volatile world we now inhabit, the era after the October 1987 debacle, it is apparent that even the best companies, the ones with the highest rankings and credit ratings, the ones with the most conservative balance sheets, the ones with stellar product lines or services, can all be affected by a dramatic selloff in the market or by exogenous (outside) factors, as the economists are fond of calling them. If you panic and sell out at the wrong time, you can indeed be hurt.

It cannot be reiterated often enough that investing is a long-term affair; it is generally wise to sell (or buy) when you want to, when a goal has been achieved or some sound decision dictates that it is time to sell. If you are forced to sell or are panicked into selling, you are likely to be at a disadvantage.

Investing for safety sharply reduces the universe of stocks for you to consider. Growth stocks, for most part, are not likely to qualify, small capitalization over-the-counter stocks, with a few exceptions, are out, and the whole tier of listed secondary issues must be culled very carefully. What's left?

There are between 100 and 200 industrial categories, depending on how you wish to define them, from advertising to wire-and-cable companies. Safety lies in the one or two top companies in each group. Another way of ensuring safety is to invest only in the Dow Jones components, since they are generally the largest and most broadly held companies in the country. They did indeed fall dramatically in the 1987 crash, but recovered in the following year. That approach naturally limits one to a relatively few issues.

The S&P 100 is a broader list of some of the better companies, but it is not a tool for stock selection and some of the issues have had anything but a safe record. However, you can use the S&P rankings for common stock, or that of any other service for that matter. If you invest in only the top-rated companies (those with an A+ ranking), you are likely to be reasonably secure.

For a more active approach, your potential investments should meet a number of benchmarks to be considered safe:

1. Is there a political risk? Can a simple legislative act put the business in jeopardy?
2. Is there a geographical risk? Is the company exposed by virtue of its overseas assets or earnings?
3. Is the company sufficiently large and diversified to ride out a serious business recession?
4. Has its record of growth at least outpaced the nominal growth of the gross national product, and then some?
5. Is there a consistent pattern of profitability?
6. Is the company sufficiently liquid? How do current assets relate to current liabilities?
7. Is the company's debt-to-equity ratio below average?
8. Are interest payments on outstanding debt adequately covered?
9. Are dividends adequately covered by the net earnings?

Quality businesses will respond positively to all of the above, but some special circumstance might allow for an occasional negative response. These are some of the critical measurements by which to judge whether an investment is safe. But they are not written in stone, and safety also has to do with some characteristics of a corporation which are not easily quantifiable: leadership, management, research and development, labor relations and the ability to innovate. You must also take these factors into consideration in the quest for true safety.

Y • O • U • R   M • O • V • E

- Decide how to divide your funds. What portion do you want as cash equivalents, as stocks, as bonds or other fixed-income instruments?
- Common stock holdings can be categorized three ways: for safety, for income, for growth. You must match your objectives with your risk tolerance.
- Income investors must decide whether they need monthly income or whether it is possible to wait for the semiannual payouts associated with bond holdings. Your needs will dictate the type of income investment you should purchase.
- Growth investors must search for companies that have a track record, a history of performance. Flash-in-the-pan growth can be dangerous to your portfolio.
- Safety may be in the eye of the beholder, but investors with safety uppermost in mind should look for long-established companies, ones with little debt, a long record of dividends, and a product line or service that will be in demand for the foreseeable future.

• 8 •

How To Monitor Your Portfolio

SOURCES OF INFORMATION

Investing your money should not be a full-time job—you have other things to do. It does require you to spend a few hours now and then to keep abreast of the economy and financial markets. If that commitment is not there, you should seriously consider using a professional investment counsel or a mutual fund or some other arrangement in order to provide the necessary attention. Your money is worth your time.

Investors are far better off today than they were a generation ago. Financial information was then considered too arcane for the public and most of it was dedicated to the investment community. In 1955, the average daily turnover on the New York Stock Exchange was 6 million shares; today it is 150 million.

To meet the public demand, publishers, broadcasters, statistical services, newsletter writers and an assortment of electronic data banks have stepped in to provide a plethora of information, documentation, original texts and secondary sources, as well as learned and not-so-learned commentaries on financial markets. Investors are in the happy situation of having their thirst quenched. In fact, they are in danger of being washed away by a tidal wave of information. There is, perhaps, almost too much of a good thing.

Where does one start? And more important, where does one end the quest for information? The following is a critical guide to financial information. It is far from exhaustive, and is certainly not a review of what is generally available. Rather, it is a modest compilation of sources of relevant, reliable, and generally up-to-date data.

THE BIG PICTURE

To keep you abreast of basic economic conditions, general newspapers provide national and local coverage and are especially valuable for investors in regional companies. The two major financial newspapers are *The Wall Street Journal* and *Investor's Business Daily*. *The Journal of Commerce* is more specifically designed for importers, exporters, and commodity businesses. Investors interested in foreign markets will find *The Financial Times* of London valuable. Almost every foreign country that has a stock market has a business paper, but they are usually written in the native language.

Broadcasters now supply a great deal of business information, especially on television. National television programs—CNBC/FNN, Cable News Network and the Public Broadcasting System—all provide thorough coverage of general business and market conditions.

Government publications, and especially government releases of pertinent information, are keenly awaited by the financial world—whether it be housing starts, employment figures, the money supply or crop estimates. These are picked up by the wire services and are broadcast and published immediately. But the federal government also publishes a series of monthly periodicals in which information may or may not be reported in a timely fashion.

The Commerce Department's Bureau of Economic Analysis publishes the highly regarded leading indicators and other key indicators on national income, prices and wages, employment, government activities and international transactions.

The President's Council of Economic Advisers occasionally issues newsworthy statements and publishes an especially valuable annual report. The Federal Reserve System publishes a monthly bulletin and most of the regional Federal Reserve banks publish their own monthly or bimonthly reviews, which tend to deal with specific economic questions and regional business. Most of the federal government's publications are not easy to read, but they do provide much of the information needed for a broad perspective. Happily, the key information is generally widely disseminated by the media. For example, the Fed Chairman's twice-a-year visit to Congress to deliver the required Humphrey-Hawkins testimony on employment, monetary targets and the state of the economy is considered of paramount importance and is generally reported.

Other nongovernmental agencies produce valuable reports on an occasional basis. The National Bureau of Economic Research considers whether growth of the economy has slowed sufficiently to determine (retroactively) that the nation is in a recession (following two successive quarters of no growth). The National Association of Purchasing Managers issues a monthly report, the *Purchasing Managers' Survey*, on inventory accumulation and purchasing decisions as a tool to forecast economic momentum.

The daily release of this torrent of information has a direct impact on the securities markets, but it is the weekly and monthly periodicals that place these items in perspective and give them long-term significance. The leading business and financial publications are *Barron's, Business Week, Financial World, Forbes,* and *Fortune.* In addition, virtually every industry is covered by a special trade magazine, from *Aviation Weekly & Space Technology* to the *Waste-to-Energy Report.* Academic and learned journals are valuable for background, but have little impact on the financial markets. However, periodicals such as the *Financial Analysts Journal* and the *Institutional Investor* provide seminal articles that can be illuminating.

All of these "big picture" publications serve one major purpose for the investor: to furnish an informed perspective about economic trends and business activity in the country. While it is somewhat simplistic to say that an incipient upturn in business is likely to mean higher stock prices across the board, or that the end of a business boom is likely to foretell lower stock prices, those likelihoods are borne out by the evidence from a long series of cycles.

These observations may err because they are simple, not because they are wrong. Investors will make more money if their overall timing is right rather than attempting to find great companies at the wrong time of the business cycle. Certainly, different kinds of stocks respond at different times: cyclical stocks (housing, iron and steel, chemicals, capital equipment) get their strongest impetus in the mature part of the business boom as their earnings surge. Defensive stocks (food, beverages, breweries, tobacco) do well in a period of no growth, since recessions do not impact their earnings.

As noted earlier, if you can be right with your general timing, the tide will float all boats, even the ones that aren't especially seaworthy. Understanding the current big picture is of inestimable value in selecting securities for tomorrow's markets.

An investor must then narrow his or her focus to concentrate on the markets. Markets can be in or out of sync with the general business cycle. To get a fix on it, an investor should understand the different measurements of market activity. There are a number of different averages, each indicating various aspects of the stock market.

The so-called blue chip average, the Dow Jones Industrial Average, is one of the most popular indices because it is composed of 30 of the largest, best-capitalized corporations in the country. Since the average is price-weighted, it tends to reflect the behavior of the higher-priced stocks rather than the lower-priced stocks. (If it were an unweighted average, it would reflect the percentage price changes of each security, thus giving equal value to each issue's price action.)

Originally, the DJIA could be thought of as consisting of one share from each component company. Since companies have been recapitalized, splits and stock dividends have altered the average. To compensate, the divisor has been changed; it is no longer 30, but is now below one (0.59 in 1991): a 25-point change in the average represents an actual price change of $13.98 ($0.59 \times 25$). The Dow Jones Industrial Average is heavily weighted with "smokestack" companies and does not reflect some of the more dynamic growth elements in the economy. Nevertheless, it is the one index that is most widely reported and the one that's quoted when people ask "How is the market doing?"

Standard & Poor's 500 stock index is a broader gauge of stock market activity. The companies are found not only on the New York Stock Exchange but also on the American and OTC. It is also a weighted index, but it is weighted by capitalization (the current stock price times the number of shares outstanding).

Standard & Poor's 500 index is criticized for being dominated by companies with huge capitalizations, but it does give a better picture of whether the predominant value of all the included companies is ascending or descending. Since the Standard & Poor's 500 is more reflective of the general market's behavior and the flow of investment monies, it is the index by which most professional money managers are measured. In 1976, Standard & Poor's started a smaller average of 100 blue chip companies. There is no direct correlation between the Dow Jones Industrial Average and the Standard & Poor's 100 index, but currently a move of about 7.4 points in the Dow Jones Industrial Average translates into a 1 point move in the Standard & Poor's 100. Both the Standard & Poor's 100 and 500 have options and futures contracts based on their performance and so are now closely scrutinized.

Other indices are less popular, but do reveal price behavior in special segments of the market.

- The New York Stock Exchange has its own Composite Index, an average of all 1,500 listed companies. Similar to the weighing and averaging of the Standard & Poor's 500, it uses a 1965 base of 50.
- The American Stock Exchange has a Market Value Index which is calculated somewhat differently than the other indices, but uses a 1973 base figure of 100. American Exchange listings are heavily represented by energy companies.
- The National Association of Securities Dealers Automated Quotations (NASDAQ) has a composite index, plus six sector indices, which use a base of 100 as of 1971.
- The Value Line Index, consisting of 1,700 stocks, (mostly from the New York Stock Exchange, and the rest from the American Stock Exchange), is configured as a geometric average of stock price percentage changes. Each issue carries the same weight. It is considered a more volatile index than the others. Its base period is 1967, when it equaled 100.
- The Wilshire 5,000, created in 1974, uses 1970 as its base. It consists of all the actively traded securities in the United States. It is a capital-weighted index, much like the Standard & Poor's 500, and even though most of its value comes from New York Stock Exchange

securities, the great number of OTC issues give it a more volatile character.

The Russell 3,000 tracks the most actively traded U.S. shares. The 1,000 represents the top tier, and the 2,000 represents the second tier.

With so many measurements, which one should you monitor closely? It is perhaps no surprise to find that regardless of their differences, there is great similarity in their movements and a high correlation at decisive market turns. Depending on the kind of investor you are and your objectives, you should watch the index that most closely reflects your investments. If you are interested in blue chips, the Dow Jones Industrial Average should be your guide; for a broad view, the Standard & Poor's 500; for an OTC growth portfolio, the NASDAQ is right. Whether or not the index or average is an accurate surrogate for your holdings, it is worthwhile to be aware of their action—especially moving averages that will alert you to major changes in market direction.

If your timing is right and you are ready to enter the market at the propitious time, you need some investment vehicle—ordinarily common stock. You can now invest—perhaps *speculate* is a more accurate word—in the indexes and averages through futures and options. Whether it is the Standard & Poor's 500, the NYSE Composite or the Value Line, these instruments allow an investor, for the price of the premium and/or commission fee, to take a position in the overall trend of the markets. No doubt, some people are better at projecting a future direction to the general market than they are in selecting specific businesses in which to invest. These futures and options on futures, however, are wasting instruments—expiring in 30, 60 or 90 days. (These trading vehicles will be discussed in another volume in this series, *The Basics of Speculating*.) They are not primarily for investors, but may prove of value in hedging a portfolio, as well as speculating.

If you want information about a specific company, start with the annual report. This can be obtained either directly from the company or from your brokerage house. Serious investors should not settle for the abbreviated versions published by some companies—the so-called *summary annual report*. These truncated reports do not give sufficient detail for security analysis.

The official version of the annual report, filed with the SEC, is the Form 10K. Containing all the necessary information, but no glossy photos, this is the primary source for corporate data. Most companies have a shareholder relations department that will not only send you a copy but will place your name on its mailing list for its quarterly reports (10Q) as well.

A great number of secondary sources publish compilations of financial information. Stockbrokers furnish some information—such as a stock report—from their financial and statistical services departments free of charge. But for a constant flow of information, you need to subscribe to one of these sources or make frequent use of public libraries. The major financial publishers are:

- Standard & Poor's/McGraw-Hill
- Moody's Investor Service
- Value Line Investment Survey
- Media General
- Dow Jones

Their products are too extensive to be thoroughly reviewed here, but in general they produce company reports, industry surveys for industrial, financial, utility and transportation companies, economic and financial overviews, monetary perspectives, comments on credit and the fixed-income market, reports on overseas activity and estimates on future earnings or market performance, or both.

In short, there isn't much financial information that is not covered. These services present all the hard-core data, but also go on to interpret it with extensive remarks about past company activity and future prospects. These organizations produce accurate and responsible reports, ones that are carefully researched and cautiously reported. They serve the professional investment community, but also produce shorter, summarized reports for individual investors.

Their stock-in-trade is factual information and, secondarily, opinion. The ratio is the other way around with most newsletters. There are literally hundreds of newsletters giving advice and counsel on the stock market. Most of them are published privately and require a subscription. Mark Hulbert publishes a newsletter, the *Hulbert Financial Digest*, on market letters, that ranks the performance of the model portfolios that most publications carry. He has found, among other things, that there is almost no correlation between the price of the newsletter and its performance. Newsletters, unlike the financial and statistical services, do not attempt to evaluate the whole, but frequently specialize in sectors. These range from medical technology to new issues, from utilities to overpriced securities. Their quality ranges from the sophomoric to the brilliant—a landscape that allows for considerable personal choice.

Brokerage houses also publish newsletters: some are free, some are not, depending on the size of your account. The quality is generally high, but you should be somewhat cautious about recommendations, especially if the broker is also a market maker in the issue being recommended. Furthermore, brokers and investment banking houses sometimes have investment or business relationships with corporations they assist in underwriting. It is therefore difficult, if not embarrassing, to suggest selling a stock.

One analysis of brokerage house recommendations found "buys" represented five times more often than "sells." Thus it is no secret that some of these newsletters have carried the art of salesmanship and euphemism to a new height.

COMPUTERIZED INFORMATION

With the arrival of the personal computer in the early Eighties, investors have a new tool, one which puts them on a more equal footing with large or institutional investors. It has helped in a number of ways: providing current information on economic and business news, providing instant real-time market prices and even executing transactions at the flick of a finger. Whether it is a personal computer, a dumb terminal or a word-processor with communications ability, these new data communicators put a whole new resource in investors' hands.

Most of the major statistical services, financial publishers, and electronic data vendors such as CompuServe and Genie, have electronic libraries, which, for a modest fee, provide current information. The data is transmitted through telephone lines, cable systems, or radio frequencies. Since these services are interactive, the vendors' mainframe computers respond almost instantaneously to investors' queries. They provide both fundamental financial information about a security or compare a number of issues at the same time.

In addition, if one's computer has graphic capabilities, these services will also provide line charts and volume figures, and other configurations for the technically oriented investor.

Moreover, a number of electronic publishers issue special software that is capable of downloading statistical information from a data library, and then manipulating it in some proprietary fashion, employing everything from artificial intelligence to what-if scenarios.

Clearly, this access improves an investor's ability to keep abreast of what's happening and to react accordingly. Some software systems will go so far as to monitor selected news wires and alert you to developing situations in the securities you follow. It is even possible to trade electronically with some brokerage houses as well as to do your bookkeeping and calculate your portfolio's value at the end of a day. A commitment to computerized information is not cheap, even if the connect time with data bases can be as little as $5 an hour. But for serious investors, electronic libraries are fast and reliable ways to keep abreast of the markets and the business world.

Y • O • U • R   M • O • V • E

- Access the state of the economy. Decide which stage of the business cycle the economy is in. Let your conclusions determine which mix is most appropriate. At the end of a cycle, position yourself for a defensive posture. At the start of a recovery, move to an aggressive stance.
- Besides the general commentary in the business press on the economic outlook, develop half a dozen (or more) indicators to give some structure and objectivity to your decision. For example, a recession is imminent if:
  - Interest rates climb above 10 percent
  - The discount rate is raised three times
  - Purchasing agents survey falls below the 50 percent mark
  - Leading economic indicators turn neutral
  - Gross national product growth is flat
  - Inflation is heating up and promises to accelerate

No one measurement (or series of measurements) is foolproof, but it is better to rely on evidence than on gut feeling.

- Gut feelings should not be dismissed, however. Appreciate the psychological state of the citizenry, especially investors. Without being a card-carrying contrarian, you should be put on the alert when great euphoria sweeps over the state of the economy. When everyone is making "easy" money in the market, such as in the summer of 1987, it is time to check the exits.
- At critical junctures, pay special attention to the weekly market letter of your choice and learn to read between the lines, especially if it is prepared by a brokerage house. If the technical action looks increasingly weak, prepare immediate defenses.
- Review your portfolio by reevaluating each holding. Will the particular issue hold up, both in terms of its earnings and in terms of price, should the economy turn surprisingly weak? Or should you sell it now (regardless of tax consequences) and move some of your assets into money markets and short-term Treasury bills? Are your heirloom securities still worth holding or are they becoming overripe antiques?
- Change your personal asset allocation at major turns in the economic climate and in the action of the securities markets. Regardless of whether there is an impending reason for modifying your holdings, a quarterly reexamination of them is a reasonable precaution.

• 9 •

How To Choose a
Brokerage Firm

Once you have a reasonable objective in mind and you understand the opportunities as well as the risks, it is time to find a brokerage firm with which to do business. Close to 6,000 offices of brokerage firms are member firms of the New York Stock Exchange, plus additional brokerage houses are only members of the National Association of Securities Dealers. Banks are also in the business: Some of them own brokerage houses.

Brokerage houses serve the needs of some 47 million American investors who directly own common stock plus other investments. Since one out of five citizens owns equity, you are not alone in becoming a stockholder. Indeed, the most recent survey of the New York Stock Exchange finds that the average individual investor is 44 years old, has a household income of $37,000 and owns a portfolio worth about $7,000. You don't have to be rich to enjoy people's capitalism.

DO YOU REALLY NEED A BROKER?

You can sell your home without a real estate broker and save a 6 percent commission. And you can buy and sell securities without benefit of a broker. However, the obstacles are considerable—almost insurmountable: You must find a buyer or seller for the right price and the right amount; you must authenticate the certificate (is it a forgery?); if you are buying, you must authenticate the seller (is he or she the legitimate owner?); you must determine who holds the money for the transaction while the securities are registered, and so on. In brief, it would be confusing, time-consuming and counterproductive to do it yourself.

Brokerage firms execute these transactions in markets where there are many potential participants. They generally stand behind the executions to make good on most problems that arise between buyer and seller. They keep your securities and funds in safekeeping and will guarantee their safety through government insurance. They take care of all the bookkeeping details, clip coupons and collect dividends. They provide monthly statements as to your account. They can provide information and advice. They will even lend money. And all for nominal commission charges on the order of 1 percent or less.

WHAT KIND OF BROKER IS RIGHT FOR YOU?

Up to the mid-Seventies, brokerage rates were fixed by the New York Stock Exchange. On May 1, 1975, competition finally came to the house of capitalism. Brokers had their rates deregulated and were allowed to customize their services. Negotiable rates became the order of the day. In the evolution that followed, some firms pursued institutional customers, since they were becoming such a large factor in the markets; others became research boutiques for a select group of wealthy private investors and funds; others dealt in executions off the floor of the exchanges; and some relied solely on computerized networks for activity. The large, old wire houses had a retail clientele, many storefront offices, and tens of thousands of customers. They provided a full range of financial service, but after deregulation they also tended to raise their fees.

This combination of events created a window of opportunity, and discount stock brokerage was born. The discounters discovered that many investors were both price-sensitive and averse to account executives trying to sell them issues that the firm was recommending that week.

Originally, discount brokerage was a plain-pipe-rack operation. Today they have become more elaborate, offering some of the services of a full-service broker as well. As the division between the two has narrowed, so too has the fee differential. It has become increasingly difficult to tell the two apart in some respects. Nevertheless, there are some distinct differences, which an investor should consider in making a selection.

FULL SERVICE: IS IT WORTH THE PRICE?

The full-service brokerage is a department store of financial services with a smorgasbord of products. They not only do everything in-house, they sometimes provide services for other brokers as well. Generally speaking, a full-service house will:

- Execute your transactions in the right markets at the best prices—even in foreign markets.
- Clear the execution with all its attendant paperwork.
- Provide economic information and investment research from a team of financial analysts.
- Tender investment advice on specific situations and provide personal counseling to clients.

- Offer financial management accounts that enable clients to have a money market account, checking account, bank credit card, line of credit, savings account and investment account all in one super account.

Full-service houses naturally charge for their services, as much as 2 percent for small trades. As the size of the transaction goes up, the rate falls somewhat. Good customers are offered preferred rates, and very good customers can negotiate rates. The commission schedule for a full-service firm is a computer-generated item nearly the size of a telephone directory, designed to maximize profits.

WHAT CAN DISCOUNTERS DO?

Discount brokerage is a different kettle of fish, and it is perhaps a mistake to compare a bouillabaisse with tuna salad. Bare-bones discounters offer executions and clearance—period. No advice, no information, no analysis, no foreign connections—only inexpensive trades for clients who know their own mind. Some of the more elaborate discounters do offer additional services, such as a money market fund where you can park proceeds while deciding on another investment.

For these limited services, discounters charge commission fees that may be 50 to 75 percent cheaper than the full-service houses. Commission schedules are usually simpler: They charge either a percentage of total sale or a fixed rate on the number of shares traded. Many discounters charge about 1 percent, and some will do a trade for $25 or $30.

As to which type of brokerage service is better, it is difficult to say. Even price considerations are not always comparable. Full-service houses may have an inventory of securities, especially in the over-the-counter market, and act as a broker-dealer. The net price may actually be cheaper with a full-service broker than with a discounter.

If you are an active investor and like to do your own research and develop your own ideas, you may be better served by a discounter. If, on the other hand, you are a more passive investor, are willing to listen to recommendations and find quality analysis worth paying for, a full-service house is desirable.

Trading through banks is possible, but they are usually ill-equipped to process orders quickly. Dealing with a bank simply adds another link in the paper chain, since they usually pass the order on to a brokerage firm. However, they do offer a sense of security and convenience. They hold no allure for active investors. Inactive investors may find the bank ideal for their infrequent trades.

The banks are more at home in the bond market, especially with Treasury securities. The cheapest way to buy government paper is through one of the 12 branches of the Federal Reserve System. There are no commission fees to pay, and all the details are dealt with through the Fed's book-entry system. The next best way to purchase government bills and bonds is through a bank. Depending on your business relationship, the fees range from virtually nonexistent to modest.

CHOOSING AN INDIVIDUAL BROKER

Before deciding on a full-service broker, a discounter, or even a financial service counter at the local department store or mall, you can make a more judicious and fitting choice if you bear in mind what you require and what services are provided. Also, watch out for misleading signs and downright fraudulent activities undertaken by the less scrupulous, especially some penny stock promoters. The following points should help focus your views and alert you to potential problems.

1. Make sure that the broker deals in the product of your primary interest. Do not go to a municipal bond house if you are interested in new common stock issues. The same is true for commodities or options; choose a futures broker if those are your main concern.

2. If you are made to feel uncomfortable because of the size of your account, find a retail broker that welcomes the small and medium-sized investor.

3. Has the brokerage house been through thick and thin? Can it weather hard times, and has it? Ask for their financials since they are, or should be, interested in yours.

4. Most brokerage houses are insured by the Securities Investors Protection Corporation (SIPC), a federal agency that provides insurance funded by the brokers themselves. Currently, accounts with insured brokers are protected up to $500,000 in cash and securities (with a cash maximum of $100,000). Some brokerage houses carry additional insurance, up to $2.5 million. Most member firms of national securities exchanges are required to be members of SPIC. However, this requirement does not apply to firms that are members of the National Association of Securities Dealers and do not hold clients' cash or securities. Make sure your broker is a member of SIPC.

5. Does the brokerage house have competitive margin loans should you wish to borrow money? And, conversely, do they offer money market accounts in which you can park money between investments?

6. Will they supply research information should you request any? Is the research done in-house, or do they subscribe to outside services, or do they use both?

7. Is the account executive "user friendly," or do you feel it is an imposition for him or her to answer questions? Does he or she use pressure tactics to unload new issues or the firm's stock-of-the-week?
8. Does the brokerage house promise quick and sure profits? Most respectable houses have published track records that they will happily share with you. Inevitably, there are some hits, some runs, some errors.

You must be on guard against:

1. Any cold-calling broker or financial consultant that offers you the latest and newest investment product.
2. Anyone who insists on an immediate commitment before "it's all gone."
3. Anyone who assures you that there is no downside risk (unless, of course, the subject is U.S. Treasury paper). Cold callers never try to sell government securities.
4. Any investment product that is unregulated (that is not traded on a regulated exchange). The record is unfortunately full of people who bought scotch whiskey warehouse receipts, participated in the residual waste of goldmines, and purchased other "investments" from fly-by-night operators. Organized high-pressure telephone canvassers (some even offshore) are still defrauding the public.
5. Any investment that cannot be liquidated immediately. Some investments are by their nature long-term involvements, such as real estate or limited partnerships. While an investor might well consider such investments, they probably should not constitute more than 5 to 10 percent of a portfolio.
6. Any investment that sounds too good to be true—it undoubtedly is.

TYPES OF ACCOUNTS

Once you have selected a brokerage house with which to do business, you will be asked what kind of account you wish to open. Virtually dozens of different kinds of accounts exist, for all sorts of special purposes. The following is a partial list of some of the more common accounts:

- Individual
- Joint Account with Right of Survivorship
- Joint Account with Tenants in Common
- Partnership
- Corporation
- Sole Proprietorship
- Business Trust
- Investment Club
- Trust
- Estate
- Custodian
- Community Property
- Unincorporated Association
- NonProfit/Charitable Organization
- Professional Corporation or Association
- Individual Retirement Account (IRA)
- Guardianship
- Conservatorship
- Usufruct
- Pension/Profit Sharing
- Keogh
- Self-Employed Pension

Many investors have more than one account, especially if they are using the brokerage house as a custodian for their IRA or pension account. One might also wish to separate business investments from family ones or keep spousal monies apart for legal or emotional reasons.

In recent years, the brokerage community has developed a super account—alternately termed a *cash management account,* a *financial management account* or some such variation. This all-encompassing account enables the holder to do virtually all brokerage and banking within the account. It provides checks on the account; a credit card or travel and entertainment card, or both; a money market account for parked money; and a provision for lending money against the account's assets. This margin lending is available, either to buy grand pianos or additional securities.

Most investment accounts are *cash accounts,* that is, all transactions are done for cash and are subsequently settled within five business days. If there is no credit balance in your account, you are expected to pay for your purchases within that time, and conversely you can expect to be paid from sales in a similar time.

It is possible to open a *margin account* to buy on credit. The minimum cash requirements for a margin account differ from broker to broker, but in general they expect an initial deposit of $2,000 to $3,000. Margin regulations are primarily set by the Federal Reserve System as part of their financial controls over credit. Margin requirements have not changed since 1974. They are now set at 50 percent—that is, you can borrow half the amount of the purchase from the brokerage house. Should you wish to buy $10,000 worth of stock, you need only put up $5,000. The other $5,000 will be lent to you. The rate of interest on a margin loan is determined by both the prevailing interest rates and the size of your account. Larger accounts can obtain better rates. Brokers borrow in turn from banks at what is termed the *call money rate,* a figure published in the business section of your newspaper.

Margin loans are one of the cheapest forms of borrowing, about one percentage point over the prime rate and, as previously noted, need not be used exclusively for purchasing securities. There is no paperwork, other than establishing the margin account, and no questions are asked.

There are, of course, some drawbacks to a margin loan, since these loans are essentially a form of demand loan. It is here that the second margin regulation, one required by the New York Stock Exchange, comes into play. The federal requirement is 50 percent as an initial requirement, but brokerage houses must protect their loan by requiring that the investor's equity represent at least 30 percent of the current market price of the stock. This rule protects the broker's loan; remember, he or she is a lender, not a co-participant, in your investment decisions.

Should the value of your investment fall below the 30 percent figure, you will receive a margin call—a telegram or telephone call—requesting additional cash (or securities that can be margined) to bring up your depleted account to maintenance level. If you cannot, or decide not to meet the margin call, the broker will "cover the call," that is, sell sufficient stock to meet the need. In short, if $10,000 worth of stock (say, 200 shares at $50) fell in value to $3,000 (the 200 shares are now worth only $15 apiece), the account would be on the verge of violating maintenance margin. Margin investing is a risky technique, covered in detail in *The Basics of Speculating*.

With a cash account, you can take delivery of the securities you bought should you wish to. Most investors leave their stocks and bonds with their brokers, especially now that they are insured. This facilitates trading, since the investor is saved the trouble of running to safe deposit box and post office. Securities left with brokerage houses are termed to be in *street name*, that is, in the custodial care of the broker.

While the disposition of securities is optional in cash accounts, it is obligatory—if you have a margin account—to keep the stock with the broker, since it is the collateral for the loan. In addition, the broker can loan the stock to others who might execute short sales.

It is important to decide whether you wish to give your account executive or registered representative (or anyone else for that matter) limited trading authority. Such power would enable the broker to buy or sell securities in your name without consulting you. Obviously, this is a matter of trust, one that no doubt will grow from experience and track record. The cautious stance, initially, would be not to grant such power. Should the relationship grow smoothly and the broker's recommendations and explanations of what is happening in the markets prove accurate and reasonable, then you might reconsider giving the broker limited trading authority.

While most trading and investing activity continues without incident and problems, they occasionally crop up. Unexecuted orders, orders executed at the wrong price, purchases (or sales) that were never agreed to, securities that were totally inappropriate for the investor—these are just some of the problems that occasionally arise. The most serious conflicts, those of fraud and deceit, will be handled by the courts. However, it should be understood that clients agreeing to trade through a member firm of the New York Stock Exchange give up the right to legal proceedings in general commercial conflicts with their brokers. When they open their accounts, they agreed to arbitration rather than litigation. This has been upheld in cases that have gone all the way to the Supreme Court. The arbitration proceedings are relatively simple and can be initiated by a simple claim statement and a nominal processing fee.

The securities industry is largely self-regulating, as mandated by Congress. Most member firms have compliance departments to see that both state and federal laws are obeyed. An individual investor can, of course, bring a complaint to the SEC, but unless it is a major problem concerning such factors as insider trading, fraud or unregistered securities, the SEC is not likely to do much other than refer the problem to one of the self-regulating agencies.

TRADING ORDERS

An active investor will find it profitable to understand and use the variety of market orders found in daily operations. They can save money in executing orders and defend a portfolio in turbulent weather.

All orders obviously contain some vital information such as the name of the company and the class of securities (class A, preferred stock, etc.). What is the size of the order? Is it a *round lot* (in denominations of 100) or an *odd lot* (less than 100 shares)? Are the shares to be bought (a *long position*) or disposed of (a long position or a short sale)?

Since you are not likely to buy or sell on the spur of the moment, you are no doubt familiar with the trading patterns or parameters within which the shares trade. Having watched the bid (a price at which market makers will buy from the public) and the asked (a price at which market makers will sell), it becomes clear what the market price is at a given moment. You can attempt to control the actual transaction price by using price limits and time limits.

Market Order

If you are anxious about price movement, you can put an order in "at the market." Unless some dramatic news affects the price between the broker's quotation of the real or actual market, and the execution of a market order (usually executed within a minute or so of when it is given), you will receive either the bid or asked price, depending which side of the transaction you are on. The *market order* is executed as soon as it reaches the floor of the exchange, and at the best possible price.

Limit Order

If, on the other hand, you wish to achieve a certain price and you foresee no immediate news to affect the price outside of its normal trading range, you might place a limit order on the transaction. A *limit order* simply states that you will not pay more than your stipulated price if you are buying, or receive less if your are selling. Since the limit order is likely to be removed or away from the actual market price, you will have to await its execution if it is to be done at all. Thus a *limit order* has to be marked as to whether it is to stand for a day, a week or a month, or whether it is to be good until canceled (GTC)—an open order. You may receive an even better price, depending on the vagaries of the market, but in no event will you receive a worse one.

Special Orders

Other types of orders have largely to do with special circumstances. The most common is a *stop order*, sometimes called a *stop-loss order*)—a pending order that is executed when the market price equals or passes through the given price. For example, suppose you bought stock at $15 that has risen to $25. You want to protect your gain, or much of it. A properly set stop sell order, say, 10 percent below the highest price, does not disturb your position. You enter a stop sell order to sell at $22.50. Should the stock price continue to rise, you benefit from the continued strength. If it should weaken and touch $22.50, your stop order immediately becomes a market order to be executed.

Some investors enter stop orders when they initially buy shares, setting the limit at 7, 10 or 15 percent below the buy price. This strategy immediately sells them out of the security if the market goes against them. Stop orders should be used with great discretion, since they can sell out a position that is simply being buffeted by normal market fluctuations. Tight stop orders may do more harm than good, but they are a useful tool in safeguarding profits from a sudden and unexpected piece of bad news. With stop orders there is no guarantee that you will obtain that price should some disaster befall the issue. The price might drop away before the stop order can be executed.

Other special orders are useful for particular circumstances and timing. *On open* requires the order to be executed when the market starts trading; *on close* requires the order to be executed at the last price for the day; *fill or kill* requires that the order be executed immediately; all or none requires that the whole order be executed or none of it be done.

Because odd-lot transactions are trades of less than 100 shares, they typically carry an extra charge, known as the odd lot differential. Typically, the odd lot differential is 1/8 point on the NYSE, but 1/4 point on the American Stock Exchange for stock selling over $40. That differential is subtracted from or added to the effective price that is usually the first round lot sale after the order was received. For example, if the last sale was $50 per share in a round lot, the purchaser will have to pay $50.25 a share for the odd lot. Some firms do not charge a differential, especially if they have a substantial odd lot department. If the firm has the shares in inventory, it may deal with a customer on a net basis, which makes the transaction less expensive.

SHORT SALES

A short sale is the sale of securities one does not own, on the presumption that the stock is overvalued. Instead of following the market maxim of buying low and selling high, the short seller first sells high and then buys low. To execute a short sale, the seller borrows the stock from a broker, promising of course to return it at a later date.

The short seller's assumption is that the inflated security will fall in price when it is recognized that there is less there than meets the eye—e.g., sales of the new widget are bound to fall off, a new competitor is on the horizon, the key management or research people are leaving, high interest rates are sure to hurt earnings. Whatever the reason, the short seller hopes to replace or to cover the short position when prices drop.

Short positions make most investors uncomfortable, even though markets go down almost as often as they go up. If you own a long position of AT&T, the worse-case scenario, however improbable, would see the shares' value fall to zero. If you had a round lot of Telephone, bought at $40, you would loose $4,000.

When you sell short, however, your exposure is infinite. Instead of falling, the shares of the telephone company bound ahead. The price of the shares might climb to some astronomic level and you may be forced to buy in or cover at far higher levels. At $80, the short seller has lost $4,000. A buy stop order set, say 10 percent above the sale price or $44, would have saved the seller from such an embarrassing situation.

This kind of order would also protect the short seller from having to put up more cash should the market price advance. Borrowed stock must be secured 100 percent at all times. If the loan does not cover the full value of the sale, additional funds must be deposited with the lender of the stock. Limit orders would reduce that exposure, but of course would act to end the short position.

Short sales can be used for other purposes. A short sale can be a hedge. It is possible to short blue chip stocks so that a general market downturn will not leave him or her completely exposed. In recent years, selling or buying futures indices have replaced the short sale as a cheaper and broader hedge.

Some investors use short sales as a tax device, one that pushes the tax consequence of a transaction into the following year. You can lock in a profit in one year by selling an equal amount of shares short to match your long position. Once the new year has started, you deliver the shares originally bought to the lender of the shares you borrowed and sold short. This is called a short sale against the box (a safety deposit box in which the shares are presumed to reside).

Though most investors do not feel comfortable with short sales and their unlimited exposure, fundamental security analysis should be every bit as valuable in divulging the overvalued, hyped and promoted companies as it will in revealing the undervalued, discrete and unrecognized issues. Whether you wish to play on that side of the court is matter of personal taste.

It is, however, worth observing some of the short sale indicators, as noted previously, for both their technical and psychological implications. Large short positions (this information is compiled and published on a monthly basis) indicates a fair amount of skepticism about the company's prospects, but also tends to put something of a floor under the stock. Any buying in the stock causes the shorts to cover, thereby causing further upside pressure.

The psychological or sentiment indicators for short sales are based on exchange specialist short sales, exchange member short sales, the short interest ratio and odd-lot short sales. Since specialists are charged with maintaining orderly markets, their intimate knowledge of the stocks they trade and the order book on those stocks gives them an insight as to the risk-reward ratio at certain price levels.

The specialist short-sale ratio is measured by dividing the total volume of short sales into the total volume of specialists short sales (as reported weekly). Should the ratio be 40 percent or less, the specialists are bullish, betting that a rally will shortly occur. Anything more than 65 percent is bearish, showing that the specialists are covering their positions for a precipitous selloff. Member short sales show similar insights into the market direction. The more general short interest ratio is derived by dividing the short interest, the number of shares sold short on the NYSE, by the average volume for the month. When that indicator rises above 150 percent it is considered bullish, and below 100 percent is bearish.

Finally, the odd lot short sales to purchase, the odd lot ratio, is presumed to be an indicator of what the small, uninformed investor is doing. Since the belief has long existed that the small investor is always wrong at critical junctures, the ratio is a contrary indicator. If the small investor is heavily shorting the market, this is considered bullish. The odd lot short sales ratio is figured by dividing odd lot short sales by the total odd lot sales. If the ratio exceeds 3 percent, the indicator is bullish, and when it declines below 1 percent the reading is bearish. Recent studies show that the small investor is not so wrongheaded as was once believed. Perhaps this last indicator should be viewed with some skepticism.

Y·O·U·R   M·O·V·E

- Consider your needs in selecting a brokerage firm. If you do your own homework and spend a great deal of time in analyzing the market, you may find the full-service broker an expensive indulgence. If on the other hand, you wish to keep in touch with what leading analysts are thinking and writing, a connection with a major investment banking firm is certainly worthwhile.

- Compare cost structures of the discounter and a full-service broker. If you execute only a few trades a year, the difference may not be great. If you trade frequently, however, the difference may determine whether your activity is profitable.

- Use market orders to obtain the best executions. They provide a discipline, restraining you from the impulse to buy before the price moves away. Stop orders are especially useful in locking in profits.

- Even if you are constitutionally against selling short, observe what the short sellers are doing, especially in your stocks. The buildup of large short positions can be a warning of impending trouble.

- Regard the specialists' short-sale ratio, their short sales against total short sales. Specialists are always short in order to conduct an orderly market, but when their volume increases markedly, it may be an early warning signal of lower markets.

Epilogue

There is only one reason to invest—to make money, but that is the end result of a long and complex process.

When asked what the market will do, J. P. Morgan's oft-quoted classic response was that "it will fluctuate." The fluctuations might be considered as waves on the surface of the ocean. The forces that propel the waves are the economic drives inherent in our modern society.

The main reason for investing is not to profit by the transitory ups and downs of the waves, but to partake in the underlying forces of growth that propel those waves. The securities markets are a reflection of those forces. Perhaps the most significant aspect of the American economy is its long history of robust growth. There have been recessions and depressions along with the booms. But because of the natural resources of the country and the innovation of its people, the American economy was, and remains, a remarkable engine for creating wealth, raising the standard of living and providing profits and surpluses for its citizens.

In the 1980s the nation went through a rough period with the spread of the rust belt, deindustrialization, foreign competition, trade imbalances, declining value of the dollar and a fall in productivity. Simultaneously, it has retrofitted a number of industries, created a huge service sector, achieved almost full employment and decontrolled, deregulated and revitalized some hitherto hidebound aspects of the economy.

Astute investors can make substantial returns on their money if they properly and accurately discern the underlying movements of the business cycle. Indeed, understanding the business cycle may be one of the most important concepts for the potential, as well as the sophisticated, investor.

Beyond the business cycle, investors must structure a portfolio that meets the personal objectives of safety, income and growth. It is important to get the mix right, to achieve a balance of what are sometimes conflicting needs.

Once the equilibrium is found, you must select the most appropriate securities to fill the niches. That is no easy job, considering the deluge of conflicting advice. Opposing views after all that make markets convince some people to buy and others to sell.

Investors can safeguard their portfolios if they discipline themselves to follow the criteria that they themselves establish. If you are hesitant to trust your own judgment, are indecisive, or simply cannot spare the time, then either hire a professional to manage your funds or employ a management company that administers a divergent family of mutual funds.

We have already examined some of the important criteria for stock selection, but they bear repeating. Look for the following when considering a stock purchase:

1. A history of steadily rising earnings—a growth rate of at least 7 percent strongly suggests that earnings will double in ten years.
2. A dividend payout that indicates that management is eager to share the rewards of growth with the stockholders.

3. A price/earnings ratio that is not more than that of the DJIA or S&P's 500, and preferably much less—perhaps about 7.
4. A return on equity that is relatively constant, with an upward bias; a target of 5 percent is not unreasonable.
5. A book value that is below the market price.
6. A current ratio that is over 2.
7. A debt-to-equity ratio that does not exceed 1/3, but no debt is better still.
8. A technical pattern of a stock price that appears ready for an upward breakout after a long period of consolidation.
9. Confirmation of the technical pattern by increased volume.
10. A skilled, hands-on management, producing goods or services that in some ways are special and not likely to be made obsolete or irrelevant.

If those are some of the criteria for buying, when should you sell securities? In some ways that is just as difficult a decision, but no less important.

1. Sell when the stock's price is not acting the way you had anticipated. Put either a mental stop order or a real sell stop order at 10 percent below its purchase price.
2. Sell if any of the underlying fundamentals change markedly, or if you suspect that they are about to change.
3. Sell if the technical pattern of the stock starts to deteriorate. Be on guard if the volume increases, but the price remains unchanged.
4. Consider selling a portion of your portfolio if a general recession appears on the horizon, especially the weaker issues. Keep the stronger issues and the interest-sensitive securities.

5. Consider selling a portion of your portfolio if inflation accelerates and interest rates move significantly higher.
6. Sell if the stock has met your target objectives, but the future looks cloudy. Don't sell if a rosy scenario is still the dominant view.
7. Sell some issues to reposition your capital if the tax code changes and capital gains are taxed at levels lower than ordinary income.

You should not overlook new trends and innovative technologies, though they may not meet all your investment requirements. There should be some room in your portfolio for tomorrow's developments. In the 1990s, America will continue to experience an explosion of new products, a tidal wave of new services.

Generally speaking, new companies are not investments, but speculations. They sell on hope, dreams and fantasy—not on such mundane matter as book value, profit margins, quarterly earnings or dividend yields. In brief, investors do not purchase these securities by the ordinary processes of security analysis. Nevertheless, these companies may discover the next landmark innovations in energy, office communications, cardiac disease, birth control and famine relief. The list of one-time small innovative companies that have succeeded are well-known in the annals of finance: Polaroid (instant photography), Xerox (photocopying), Apple (personal computing) and MCI (non-Bell telephonics), among others.

Investors may miss some of the excitement by avoiding research and development companies, and no doubt many prefer the attitude of not-in-my-portfolio. Since the odds are largely against new companies, investors should have no more than 5 to 10 percent of their holdings in such businesses.

Finally, investors should be aware of what commonly goes wrong. Everyone makes investment mistakes, and the following are some of the more obvious ones.

1. Trading too frequently eats up commission fees before a situation has had a chance to prove itself.
2. Responding to rumors, tips and gossip passed off as inside information.
3. Buying on impulse before investigating the situation.
4. Giving discretionary power to a broker before the broker has established a sound record of recommendations.
5. Responding to high pressure salespersons soliciting "no-loss" investments.
6. Chasing the highest dividend yields without realizing that high yields are more often a sign of trouble than a sign of opportunity.

There are always some Chicken Little characters who are sure that the sky is falling. However, the overall performance of the United States—irrespective of the natural volatility that is to be expected in a market-driven economy—is admired and envied around the world. The 1990s promise to be just as exciting and just as profitable as other periods of growth. This is bound to be assisted by the spread of democracy in Eastern Europe and the Pacific Rim.

Since the founding of the New York Stock Exchange in 1792 under a Wall Street Buttonwood tree, investors have handsomely participated in the nation's growth. They will now no doubt benefit from the rejuvenation of the domestic economy and the expansion of the global one.

Glossary

acid test ratio The value of cash, notes and accounts receivable divided by the current liabilities. This measurement of corporate liquidity, known also as the quick asset ratio, should be at least 1:1 to be considered satisfactory for corporate credit requirements.

advance-decline line A ratio of the number of issues advancing against the number declining.

asked price Also called the offer, this is the lowest price at which a holder is willing to sell his security at a given time.

assets All a corporation's property such as plant, equipment and cash. The fixed assets are the buildings and machinery. The intangible assets are patents, copyrights, trademarks and goodwill. Current assets are the sum of cash, notes and accounts receivable from the sale of the product.

asset allocation The proportion of a portfolio allotted to stocks, bonds and cash.

beta A mathematic measurement of a stock's sensitivity to the movement of the general market. A beta of 1 means that the stock moves in line with the market, but a beta of 1.5 means that it is 50 percent more volatile on the upside than the general market.

bid price The highest price that a buyer is willing to pay for a security at a given time.

bond A secured promissory note that represents the issuer's pledge to pay back the principal at face value on a specific date. Until that date, the issuer generally agrees to pay a fixed amount of interest at regular intervals, usually semi-annually. The term *bond* frequently is applied to other types of fixed-income instruments that technically are not bonds at all.

book value Arrived at by adding all assets, then deducting all debts and other liabilities. When this sum is divided by the number of common stock outstanding, the result is the book value per share.

business cycle The alternating phases of business conditions that range from boom to bust. A typical business cycle has five phases: revival, expansion, maturation, contraction, and recession.

call money rate The rate charged by banks to brokers for the use in margin buying by their customers.

capitalization The sum of all monies invested in a corporation and how it is divided between debt and ownership.

capital The net assets of a business.

cash flow The net income of a firm plus the amounts charged off for depreciation and other extraordinary charges.

coincident indicators Measurements of economic activity that reflect current economic conditions.

constant dollar plan A plan whereby an investor keeps a portfolio of securities at certain fixed levels by buying or selling if the proportions move substantially.

contrary investing To act against the prevailing sentiment in the stock market.

current assets *See* assets.

current liabilities *See* liabilities.

debt coverage The amount of income necessary to service the interest payments on the debt.

defensive stocks Companies producing goods and services that are little affected by the economic environment, such as food or beverages.

demand deposit Deposits in an account from which a customer can withdraw funds, either in cash or by check, upon request.

derivative instruments Financial instruments that obtain their value from some underlying securities.

discount broker   A brokerage firm that offers order executions at rates considerably lower than full-service brokers. They may or may not provide research services.

dividend payout   The percentage of dividends distributed relative to what is available from current net income.

dividend yield   The return from the common stock dividend expressed as a percentage.

dollar cost averaging   An investment plan whereby an investor invests fixed dollar sums at fixed periods of time.

Dow theory   A stock market theory that argues that business conditions are reflected in stock prices. Moreover, the theory suggest that you can predict market performance by studying the Dow Jones Industrial Average and the Transportation index based on their confirmation of each other or their divergence.

earnings per share   The net income of a corporation divided by the number of shares of common stock outstanding. This is a key ratio for determining whether the price is too high or too low in relation to other similar firms or the market as a whole.

efficient market theory   A theory about the operations of the stock market, which argues that stock prices reflect all available, relevant information. Prices adjust immediately to any new information.

full-service broker   A retail brokerage firm that offers execution of securities orders, as well as research and other services.

fundamental analysis   An examination of the company through its income statement and its balance sheet in order to determine its health.

income statement   The profit and loss statement of a business for a fixed period of time.

index funds   Mutual funds whose composition mirrors one of the major stock market indices.

index arbitrage   A technique employed by institutional investors to profit from the small discrepancies between the stock market and the futures markets.

intrinsic value The price a security should sell at when properly priced in the marketplace. Intrinsic value is sometimes termed *investment value.*

lagging indicators A series of economic measurements that trail current business conditions.

leading indicators A series of economic measurements that foretell business conditions.

leverage The use of borrowed funds in order to increase one's position in a security.

liabilities All claims against a business, whether current or in the future.

long A long position indicates that you own the security.

margin call A demand by the brokerage house for additional funds from a customer to meet the minimum requirements set by the firm. A decline in the stock price has reduced the customer's equity value. To protect its loan, the broker demands more collateral, either in cash or marginable stocks.

market order An order to buy or sell securities at a price prevailing when the market reaches the trading floor. There are different orders to ensure for the proper entry or exit, such as a sell stop order. This order is activated when a trade is done at or below the order price.

moving average A mathematical technique for measuring small fluctuations to reveal a general trend.

odd lot An odd lot of shares is from 1 to 99 shares. An odd lot is slightly penalized when an order is executed, compared to a round lot, usually 100 shares.

program trading Computer generated trading by institutions in order to profit from the differentials between baskets of common stock and equal amounts of futures contracts.

quick ratio A ratio between liabilities and current assets. It indicates a company's ability to pay off its liabilities with available cash.

random walk theory A stock market theory which implies that there is no discernible pattern to stock prices. In brief, past prices do not predict future price action of securities.

return on equity A business's net income, divided by the stockholder's equity.

return on investment The amount earned from the capital invested. This is usually expressed as a percentage.

round lot 100 shares of stock is the regular trading unit in the equity market.

short An investor who sells securities in the anticipation of repurchasing them at lower prices.

specialist An exchange member who is charged with maintaining an orderly market in a security and, if necessary, to buy and sell for the specialist's account to stabilize the market.

technical analysis The study of a stock's price action in order to determine its future movements.

time deposit A bank account that has a future maturity date. Customers cannot withdraw funds from a time deposit without usually being penalized.

volume The total number of shares traded. This is a technical indicator, which helps confirm price action of a given security.

Index